Awakening the New Masculine

The Path of the Integral Warrior

Awakening the New Masculine

The Path of the Integral Warrior

A Psychospiritual Journey into Fullness for Men

Gary Stamper, PhD

OPEN BOOK
EDITIONS
A Berrett–Koehler Partner

Awakening the New Masculine
The Path of the Integral Warrior

iUniverse books may be ordered through booksellers or by contacting:

iUniverse
1663 Liberty Drive
Bloomington, IN 47403
www.iuniverse.com
1-800-Authors (1-800-288-4677)

ISBN: 978-1-4697-3150-6 (sc)
ISBN: 978-1-4697-3151-3 (e)
ISBN: 978-1-4697-3153-7 (hc)

Library of Congress Control Number: 2012900548

Printed in the United States of America

iUniverse rev. date: 3/2/2012

Endorsements

"Awakening the New Masculine is a brave, exciting and significant contribution to one of the most important aspects of our time—the birth of a New Sacred Masculine capable of being fiercely and tenderly protective of the world and human life."—Andrew Harvey, Author of *The Hope a Guide to Sacred Activism*

"Gary Stamper's vision of the new integral man is a refreshing departure from mythic visions of the past, but without abandoning their power or magic." — Allan Combs, author of *Consciousness Explained Better* and *The Radiance of Being*

"Something very ancient and very new is being presented here! Gary Stamper is bringing together many disciplines, much experience, fine scholarship, and good writing style too." — [Fr.] Richard Rohr, O.F.M. Center for Action and Contemplation, Albuquerque, NM (Author of *Wild Man to Wise Man* and *Adam's Return*)

"Awakening the New Masculine: The Path of the Integral Warrior is a call to all men everywhere to pay attention to the powerful evolutionary forces that are waking up and being activated at this pivotal time of change on planet Earth. Gary Stamper has done a masterful job of pulling together various integral and visionary shamanic approaches to assist the change that is greatly needed for not only men of all ages but also for the masculine that is ready to be activated within us all." — Linda Star Wolf, author of six books, including *Visionary Shamanism: Activating the Imaginal Cells of the Human Energy Field*

"Gary Stamper has woven many strands together into a strong and flexible fabric. He combines Integral theory, Archetypal Psychology, and men's issues into a readable, useful book with real practical value. This cogent and intelligent book describes the evolving masculine in a way that educates without being preachy, and encourages inner development without resorting to cheerleading or ego stroking. It speaks the truth about men and masculinity, then offers practical step-by-step processes that a man, or group of men, can use to move toward greater integrity, balance, and fullness. If you're already committed to your own self development, read this book. If you're new to men's work, this book is a great place to start." —Lion Goodman, *Director of Men's Programs, The Shift Network, Author of "Menlightenment: A Book for Awakening Men"*

"Viva la evolución! Gary Stamper's ability to synthesize multiple memes of the evolutionary urge is admirable -- and right on time. As we often say in MKP, the 'journey continues'. The Integral Warrior series that are outlined here fills in gaps that MKP's 48 hour New Warrior Training Adventure isn't designed to handle. I believe these next steps in growth are essential to battle the demons we face as a society. In the last three years, I've seen more and more synchronicity in the world of transformative work with the sacred masculine and feminine. The convergence of sacred activism, integral theory, somatic practices (like Shamanic Breathwork), and Jungian mythopoetics is, for me, the cutting edge. It's a frightening and spectacular time to be a man, the possibilities for partnership, transcendence, and integration are stunning. The Integral Warrior sees the trees, and the forest, and the paths. If you're hearing the call to a new initiation, this book might look more like a map."—Boysen Hodgson, MKP USA Communications Director

What Men Are Saying

"This process helped me get in touch with my fears around stepping into leadership roles in my life. Now that I have a full grasp of my internal process, I am much less apprehensive about taking on leadership tasks and find myself to be much more proactive in all aspects of my life! I highly recommend taking advantage of the Integral Warrior process that Gary so brilliantly facilitates!" — Chuck W., Asheville, NC

"I was able to clearly define my own weaknesses and struggles that appear whenever the warrior in me is repressed. Going much deeper than Mankind Project work, Gary also guided us through a study of the states and stages of masculine development in order to discover our deepest purpose and our mission. Gary is one of the most powerful facilitators that I have ever met. He was able to eloquently and artfully provide the framework for tracking the historical evolution of the world's cultures, from primitive man to the present, and show how it applies as well to organizations and individuals. And he brings his own gold—integrity, humility, and the openhearted gift of his mission—to the weekend."

"For me, the workshop was the perfect blend of the cognitive (with the stimulating discussions about how individuals and cultures move from one level of consciousness to the next) and experiential (with the Shamanic journeys that he led with an almost hypnotic intensity). A final ritual ceremony (which we designed ourselves) allowed me to declare my ownership of the warrior archetype and all of its shadows."
— Larry B., Cincinnati, OH

"There has never been a better method of shaking the old paradigm to its foundation or of unleashing the true or new masculine the way that Gary does. He brings it! I feel more complete and whole as a person and more important to myself and loved ones. As a man, the process of integrating various aspects of masculinity is overdue. I feel like a fish that has been put back in the water, able to see other aspects that were invisible before the transformation into the integral warrior. Now I'm able to breathe for the first time as an awakened integrated soul thanks to Gary and the process he's created. If you're looking to expand your awareness and grow, this is the process for you." — Robert M., Whittier, NC

"Here is what has changed since, during, and as part of my participating in the Integral Warrior process: Prior to going through the process, I was out of balance—my King knew it, my Lover was suffering and withdrawn, and the Magician had run out of tricks. I was basically in Warrior mode, and it was affecting what I was manifesting into my life. As I went through this discovery process with you and my new brothers, I gradually realized that. Using the tools you brought, I eventually saw that I was missing the point. I gave into my life's purpose … or at least rediscovered it! Here is a quote of mine that was recently published by a young man who conducted an online survey asking what my operating beliefs are. I would never have said this two years ago. 'Be amused!' If we take ourselves and our world too seriously we all suffer in fear and depression. We all love a good laugh; it makes us feel good. When we feel good, we are at our best, and when we are at our best we can overcome all of life's challenges. So, I now have a running internal dialogue that focuses more on how I can 'choose' to be pissed off at what goes on in everyday life—or see how amusing it all really is. 'I speak my truth' has become much easier—I now realize that when I don't speak my truth, whatever it was that I was avoiding would keep showing up. Funny, isn't it! I share more deeply—with my loved ones and with perfect strangers. It makes for a brighter day, and all it takes is a kind word or compliment. And yes, I laugh more easily. I've always had a great sense of humor—I just misplaced it for a long while. Thanks, Gary. I worry less." — Carl G., Cincinnati, Ohio

"Gary is clearly an inspired leader of the Integral Warrior/Shamanic Priest Process. His knowledge and openness are matched by his humor and centeredness/balance. What he is, he imparts. Afford yourself the gift of this journey."

"Gary is a joyous, open, and willing spirit who brings a wealth of knowledge and experience to the Integral Warrior process, which consists of a group of men intimately relating to one another in a loving and sharing that can open new vistas from within."

"Gary is dedicated to a purpose and a process, very knowledgeable, considerate, and dedicated to creating a more harmonious, livened, enlightened … existence on Earth. I would definitely recommend this process to other men."

"I look forward to continuing this work with you and whoever else you may enlist."

"You and the Integral Warrior process took me deeper than I thought I could go. I now see some of the places I need to work on and look forward to continuing to do this work with you."

"I have always been wary of what I call 'woo-woo' new age mysticism and I was a little apprehensive about attending this workshop, but it turned out to be a concise, informative, and, more importantly for me, an engaging look at some of the men's work that can improve the quality of my life. Simply put, I feel it will accelerate my growth. I strongly recommend making room for this weekend."

"You're an awesome, knowledgeable man … a skilled teacher with deep knowledge of your subject matter … and a skilled facilitator."

Acknowledgments

This book would never have been written without the pioneering efforts of innumerous men and women who came before. The book you hold in your hands is a synthesis of teachings, books, stories, groundbreaking realizations, and evolutionary processes, new and old. In an attempt to thank the people who made, and continue to make, such incredible gifts to the planet, I'll surely leave out some important ones, so let me apologize in advance. You are all in my heart.

First, the women who left me questioning why I did things the way I did, left me scratching my head, and contributed to the still-developing curiosity and wonderment that began my journey down this ever-unfolding road: my mother, Dorothy, with whom I was able to have deep conversations, and my sister, Suzy, for being the first "girl" in my life. Also, Joan, Kat, Sandy, Kelly, Sharon, Janine, Patricia, Elle, and foremost and finally, my beloved wife, Anyaa—the living embodiment of the fire of the Divine Feminine—who inspires me, challenges me, loves me, supports me, heals me, offers counsel and wisdom, and lovingly (mostly) calls me on my BS when I need it. Anyaa's work with the feminine and her Shamanic Priestess Process are what really pushed me into doing this work as a living—a passion—and helped me discover my true purpose as a man and a gift I knew nothing about.

My deepest gratitude goes out to philosopher Ken Wilber, who lit me up by articulating what I somehow already knew but did not have the words for and helped me develop a new worldview that changed my life.

I also thank my friend Allan Combs, who wrote one of my three favorite books, *The Radiance of Being*, for introducing me to Ken Wilber.

My thanks goes to SeattleIntegral, the integral salon and community I helped found and led for almost five years, for the facilitating skills I developed in leading meetings, giving me the intellectual stretch to further expand and set the integral worldview. My special thanks to cofounder Jake Werre: we dreamed and we created and had a ball doing it, didn't we?

More deep gratitude goes to Pacific Integral: my teachers Dana Carmen and Geoff Fitch; my dear friend Venita Ramirez; and especially Terri O'Fallon, who embodies the highest consciousness I've ever experienced in my life, and I'm sorry if this embarrasses you, Terri. You have no idea how you have affected my life and my approach with your wisdom, compassion, clear sight, and grace.

To author David Deida, who also literally changed my life with one book, *The Way of the Superior Man,* go my sincere thanks. Without David's visionary work, I doubt I would be doing what I'm doing or be married to the powerful woman I share my life with. Thank you for your wisdom and teaching.

To Robert Moore and Douglas Gillette, coauthors of the book *King, Warrior, Magician, Lover,* for the deeper exploration into the mature masculine Jungian archetypes that shape our lives and for providing a road map for boys to become authentic men that is such a huge part of the Integral Warrior workshop series. Men owe so much to you.

To Richard Rohr, who expresses the importance of initiation and ritual better than anyone I know.

I also want to express my gratitude and love to, first, my friend Brad Collins for the Priest Process workshop, which shaped the foundation and evolution of the Integral Warrior workshop and this book, and, second, to Linda Star Wolf, who, with her husband Brad, founded the community where Anyaa and I live and built our home, for the parent organization of Venus Rising: A Church and a University, and the home of the Shamanic Breathwork™ Process, the powerful experiential process that allows the ego to get out of the way of what the soul wants to call forth. This book began as a PhD thesis through Venus Rising University, founded by Brad and Star Wolf.

Last, to all the men who have courageously and bravely stepped into the Integral Warrior workshop series to be ripped apart; face their fears, their wounds, and their shadows; die to the old and be reborn to the new in true shamanic fashion, it has been my honor and privilege to witness your transformations, to see you mature and change, to see you grasp bigger perspectives, and to see and hear your wives and partners witness and exclaim those transformations. I honor the sacred work you did in the workshop and the sacred work you take out into the world as Integral Warriors: the awakened new masculine.

for my father
Wayne Stamper 1919-2011

Introduction

With later-stage consciousness comes new awareness about the changing role of the masculine. The new masculine, this Divine Masculine, Eros, considers all other aspects, integrating and calling as many perspectives into his BE-ing as he can with fierce awareness, stretching the boundaries of what is possible, bravely holding space for the feminine, nature, body, spirit, integrity, authenticity, wisdom, and heart. The new masculine moves forward, aligning with his true purpose and the full embodiment of presence for the highest good of all beings. —Gary Stamper

IT IS CLEARLY TIME for men to wake up. Just a little over one decade into the twenty-first century, we find ourselves in the biggest struggle of our existence—a struggle in which the outcome is still unknown. It is time for men to stop acting like little boys.

No longer faced with mere territorial struggles, the consequences humankind faces today are global, and we are faced with the very real possibility of our own demise as a species. To be sure, these are issues of patriarchal power and the light and dark forces on the planet facing off against one another. It is the oldest story on the planet. It's time for the patriarchy to be disassembled and for its sons to grow up.

Never before in human history has humankind been this close to a global psychosocial and spiritual awakening. At the same time, never have we been in such danger of being swept into global totalitarianism, potentially more oppressive than any system known before. Technology, in the hands of little boys pretending to be men, has led us to this new geopolitical reality.

Never before have we been called to wake up on the scale that is required today. For the past five years, my work with men has been all about awakening the Sacred Masculine and the sacred activist within the masculine. Why men? Why not work with men *and* women? Don't the Divine Masculine and the Divine Feminine within each of us need to awaken?

This book, *Awakening the New Masculine*, and the Integral Warrior men's workshop series I've created and continue to facilitate are both predicated on the premise that there is still much healing to be done and that men, and women, almost always need to do their own work on healing their own inner masculine and feminine essences before they can ultimately come together in sacred union. We live in a culture where men have been raised and taught to compete with other men and the winner is determined by who accumulates the most. We've all seen the bumper sticker that reads, "He who dies with the most toys wins." It is in this culture of inadequate development, where most men remain boys, that men need to learn to trust other men—something we have regrettably not been taught to do. And that can only happen, I believe, within the safe container of a men's circle.

This book is about how that happens and why it's needed.

I began this journey many years ago, in my fifties, when a realization started gnawing at me that I had not contributed anything of significant value during my time on the planet. Not content with what was basically beginning to feel like a wasted life, I started searching for meaning. It wasn't that I was living a *bad* life; it was just not a very luminous life. After a couple of bad relationship experiences, I began a meditation practice on the advice of a therapist I was talking with, and something began opening for me. Having been agnostic in my spiritual beliefs since my early twenties, I found myself developing a growing spiritual awareness that soon led me to Buddhism and philosophy. The search for meaning led to bigger and bigger questions and teachers like Pema

Chodren,[1] Thomas Moore,[2] and Thich Nhat Hanh, who deepened the search that eventually led to Allan Combs (*The Radiance of Being*) and to philosopher Ken Wilber (*A Theory of Everything*).

Several years into this path, and after playing a major role in the creation and moderation of an integral salon, SeattleIntegral, I met my future wife, Anyaa McAndrew, who was doing amazingly deep women's work. Following her lead and seeing the impact she was having on women, it eventually became obvious to me that my work was going to be the mirror of hers and that one of my contributions was going to be around evolutionary masculinity. Five years of facilitating men's workshops and the creation of my workshop, the Integral Warrior, led to my PhD in shamanic psychospiritual studies and, eventually, this book.

What is the genuinely masculine contribution to the value of life, a contribution that women really cannot make? Let me quote what Matthew Fox says in his book, *The Hidden Spirituality of Men:*

> "Soul and Spirit are not the same thing. In Latin, 'spirit' (*spiritus*) is masculine and 'soul' (anima) is feminine. An awakened soul seeks spirit, but an asleep soul may distort spirit, so that spirit is all 'sky' energy with no 'earth' energy."

Fox's quote perfectly describes the loss of the indigenous heart, where men have ceased being "in love" with the earth. Spirit, also known as Eros, has become twisted and distorted, even to the point of being disowned, by dominator cultures who value dominion more than love.

In spite of this, the contribution men make is Spirit to the Soul and is "holy marriage," or *hieros gamus*, which includes an intimate union of opposites. And at this time on the planet, in the midst of the greatest shift we've ever seen, what could possibly be more important?

Western culture does not adequately support boys or men or boys becoming men. We have completely lost touch with the concept of elders as wisdom keepers, and the elders we do have were not given

---

1   Pema Chodren, *Start Where You Are* (Boston: Shambhala, 2001).
2   Thomas Moore, *Care of the Soul* (New York: HarperPerennial, 1994).

the tools they needed to become those wisdom keepers. Today, elders are burdens instead of valuable resources. Our elders have not been taught how to pass on wisdom, identities, and boundaries to the next generation. And in a society without fathers, most of us have been underfathered and overmothered. The problem, of course, is much larger than just bad fathering, although that is an issue. The bigger issue is a lack of any father or other healthy masculine influence in an age of single parents.

We've created a world of Peter Pans, or *puers*,[3] who never grow up and want to marry trophies instead of wives, and girls who want someone to take care of them instead of bold partners. "The current older generation of men, especially in the United States, has, to a great extent, not been mentored by their own fathers."[4]

They were usually given false messages from TV, movies, or worse, either in quick male style or translated through the experiences of women. Sometimes they received inaccurate and harmful information from each other. Women, with no fathers around to mentor the young, have been training boys to be their version of men, and the men who are around have not been mentored by the healthy masculine and have been modeling masculine behavior at a teenage level of development. None of these models are going to cut it when it comes to meeting the overwhelming problems we face today.

We can pass on only what we know. Men can only father their sons and daughters as far as they have gone. Men who lost their fathers at an early age may do fine with their own sons up to that age, but after that they often lose self-confidence in their parenting abilities.[5]

The levels of depression, suicides, drug abuse, alcoholism, and violence among men are all rising exponentially to the point of being staggering and frightening. Ninety-four percent of all inmates are male. Men live an average of seven years fewer than women, suffer far more from ulcers

---

3   *Puer aetrnus*, the eternal boy
4   Richard Rohr, *Adam's Return: The Five Promises of Male Initiation* (New York: Crossroad Publishing Company), 2004, p. 13.
5   Richard Rohr, *Adam's Return*, 2004.

and stress-related disease than women, and are more likely than women to die from the fifteen leading causes of death.

Over 80 percent of all suicides are committed by men. In the twenty-to-twenty-four age bracket, males commit suicide six times as much as females, and over the age of eighty-five, men are fourteen times as likely to commit suicide as women.[6]

Men Are Hurting

For over two decades, we've been told our education system favors and is based on the success of boys, but the results appear to support the exact opposite. Women are surpassing men in leadership positions, valedictorian addresses, graduation rates, jobs after graduation, and now, even salaries.[7]

In her 2010 article "The End of Men,"[8] Hanna Rosin asks what it would mean if "modern, post-industrial society is better suited to women." She then elaborates with the following:

> Earlier this year, for the first time in American history, the balance of the workforce tipped toward women, who now hold a majority of the nation's jobs. The working class, which has long defined our notions of masculinity, is slowly turning into a matriarchy, with men increasingly absent from the home and women making all the decisions. Women dominate today's colleges and professional schools—for every two men who will receive a B.A. this year, three women will do the same. Of the 15 job categories projected to grow the most in the next decade in the U.S., all but two are occupied primarily by women. Indeed, the U.S. economy is in some ways becoming a kind of traveling sisterhood: upper-class women leave home and enter the workforce, creating domestic jobs for other women to fill.

Rosin's article set off a slew of other articles: *Newsweek* Magazine's

6   National Institute of Mental Health.
7   Christina Hoff Sommers, *The War Against Boys* (New York: Touchstone, 2000).
8   *The Atlantic* Magazine, July/August 2010.

cover story two months later was titled "Man Up!" and stated that the "traditional male is an endangered species" and that it was time to "rethink masculinity." Soon after, former California governor Arnold Schwarzenegger fathered a child with a longtime member of his household staff, and Dominique Strauss-Kahn, then head of the International Monetary Fund, faced charges of rape, sexual abuse, and unlawful imprisonment—which later seem to have stemmed from mutual sex. This led Nancy Gibbs to ask in a cover story in *Time* Magazine (May 2011), "What Makes Powerful Men Act Like Pigs?"

These and numerous other articles, book, and blogs are all pointing at the same thing: Why haven't we come to terms with the crisis of modern male immaturity?

In his book *The Biology of Transcendence: A Blueprint of the Human Spirit,*[9] Joseph Chilton Pearce says we have five brains altogether and that they build on one another at years one, four, seven, eleven, and fourteen to seventeen. At each of these milestones, brain surges occur, through which all past experiences are stored and secured, or myelinated. Chilton reasons that we transcend each brain stage by being around models of higher brain functions, and if there is no modeling, neural pruning occurs and millions of brain cells die off. This is what's happening to boys of all stages who don't have the next developmental stage modeled for them.

Because postmodernism equates masculinity with patriarchy, we have, with a few emerging exceptions, been knee-deep in the quest for anything that misguidedly levels the playing field between the masculine and the feminine. Postmodernism demands that men become more like women and that women become more like men until the sacred qualities of each become flat and impotent. We have, in effect, been shamed and become ashamed of the masculine parts of who we are, and often with good reason.

But despite radical feminist denials, anger at the masculine in the past few decades, and even our doubts about ourselves, the beauty of the masculine is self-evident. We may like it, we may hate it, we tear it

---

9   Rochester, VT: Park Street Press, 2002.

apart, we dissect it, we're afraid of it, we disown it, and we push it and ourselves away. We also ignore it and take it for granted. The sad truth is that the vast majority of men have also been victims of the patriarchy.

With increasing awareness and understandable anger at centuries of patriarchal behavior, or false male power, we have come to believe that masculinity—and men—and patriarchy are the same thing. Consequently, we deny and repress the power and the gifts of the Divine Masculine.

Both men and women carry masculine and feminine energies and archetypes. When we suppress part of who we are, we cannot step into wholeness. We deny our very being, our very essence. And when we do, the shadow parts emerge.

Robert Moore and Douglas Gillette[10] have found that the characters in male myth, legend, and story—the universal images that attract men—invariably circle around four constellating images, which some call archetypes or ruling images: a king, a warrior, a lover, and a magician or wise man. These seem to be four parts of every man, our primary fascinations, the major quadrants of our souls. They challenge us, fascinate us, and threaten us, and we are unable to totally ignore them. When we try, or when we over-identify with one or another, they invariably take on a dark and compulsive nature. But the mature man honors and integrates all parts of his soul. They seem to naturally balance and regulate one another, and they make a man whole and holy. This state of being has been called the very shape of masculine holiness.

Men who go through the Integral Warrior men's process complete four initiations—calling in and claiming their king, their warrior, their lover, and their magician—so that none of them dominates the others, allowing them to balance one another in perfect masculine harmony. It has been a gift to me and my own evolution to watch the men whose processes I facilitate complete these four initiations and emerge more

---

10   Robert Moore and Douglas Gillette, *King, Warrior, Magician, Lover: Rediscovering the Archetypes of Mature Masculinity* (New York: HarperCollins, 1991).

whole, more complete, more secure, more confident, and, yes, more authentic than when they first began.

That we can initiate all four of the major Jungian archetypes is a remarkable achievement in that, historically, most cultures have affirmed only one or two parts of a man—usually the Warrior and sometimes the Magician. Very few men got to be initiated as Lovers, and even fewer as Kings. The task before us today, as Integral Warriors and Shamanic Priests, is much more difficult because we must own and validate all four archetypes, including the light and the shadow of each, letting them cook and integrate to create a full man. "Now we need enlightened and transformed Magicians, Lovers of life and beauty, and strong nonviolent Warriors to produce truly big-picture men—or Kings."[11]

In the emergence weekend, men who complete the Integral Warrior men's process self-initiate one last time, proclaiming their gift as men in service to the world. They will emerge from the process in front of their families and their friends and claim the big-picture masculine that is the birthright of every man who is willing to die to the old and be reborn to the new, as these men will have done.

Men are beginning this evolutionary process naturally, as it is required for the survival of the species. The Divine Feminine requires it so that together they can change the world in perfectly imperfect partnership through sacred union. Together they are exponentially more powerful than by themselves. The new masculine is already waking up because the planet and our survival demand it.

The path of the Integral Warrior hastens the awakening process, and not a moment too soon.

How to Read This Book

The best way to approach this book is with other men. See if you can find a group of at least three men and schedule reading individual chapters by yourselves or as a group. Then get together and discuss the concepts, the teachings, and the practices. Take turns facilitating the

---

11   Richard Rohr, *Adam's Return*, 2004.

meetings and the practices. What resonates with you? What makes you feel uneasy? Why? Try to go as deep with one another as possible, and be as real and authentic as you can with your discoveries, your attractions, and your "dis-ease" with the subject matter.

Hold one another accountable for not being true to yourselves, not being authentic. Call BS on men who don't go deep enough or who try to "get away" with less than their best. Ask the other men to hold you accountable for living "at your edge" and just a little beyond, for attending meetings, for contributing. This is where the growth is. Read and discuss with other men who are serious about wanting real change in their lives, who aren't making excuses or blaming others. When they do, call them on it.

Last, take responsibility for your own personal and spiritual evolution, and have fun doing it. It will be incredibly rewarding.

CONTENTS

Chapter 1: What's Wrong with Men? Pathways to Healing the Masculine

Masculine or feminine, we have all been wounded by our primary caretakers, by our culture, and by each other. The premise of this book is that we not only can heal our wounds but *must* heal them in order to reach more awakened states of being, or what is sometimes called later-stage consciousness. That healing happens largely around exploring, revealing, and bringing forth awareness of what stops us from emerging into the powerful beings we know we can become. What gets in our way and prevents us from realizing our full potential in our work, our relationships, and our peace are our reactive and asleep selves, our shadows.

What is the work that needs to be done on the planet at this time to heal the deep wounds of the masculine and feminine? Following the lead and the work of my partner and wife, Anyaa McAndrew,[12] one of my gifts to the world is the healing of the postmodern masculine. Her work revolves around helping postmodern women who have become overly "masculinized" to reclaim their more powerful, integrated feminine, which includes the masculine. My work revolves around helping postmodern men who have become overly "feminized"—something that needs to happen—to reclaim the healthy aspects and fullness of the new masculine without shame and with a strong sense of their purpose and a clear sense of their sacred mission, while still maintaining their

---

12   http://www.goddessontheloose.com

healthy feminine. It is the complete integration of the masculine and feminine that allows men and women to step into a richer fullness.

Before we look at the new masculine, let's take a look at where the men's movement began and where it's been. Then we can take a look at where it might be going. By no means is this a comprehensive look at the men's movement; it's an overview.

Oddly enough, it may have been the movie *Field of Dreams* in 1989 that set the tone for the men's movement. According to Frank Pittman, the author of *Man Enough: Fathers, Sons, and the Search for Masculinity*, most women (his statement, not mine) thought it was a "dumb fantasy" about baseball. "But baseball, with its clear and polite rules, and all its statistics, and its players who are normal men and boys rather than oversized freaks, is a man's metaphor for life. *Field of Dreams* did amazing things to grown men, who soaked themselves in sobs. Some couldn't walk out of the theater when the movie was over. The theme in this or any other movie that draws the most tears from grown men is unquestionably the lifetime mourning for the father they couldn't get close to."[13]

Another of our central myths is that of the son who could not get his father's approval so he turned violent and killed his brother—familiar as the story of Cain and Abel.

Other movies that carry similar themes are *East of Eden* (1995), the coming-of-age trilogy *Star Wars* (as in *Hamlet* or *Iron John*), *The Godfather*, and the third film of the *Indiana Jones* series, in which Sean Connery, as the father of Jones, shows even more masculine bravado than Indiana Jones himself.

The Mythopoetic Men's Movement

With the international best-selling book *Iron John: A Book about Men*, Robert Bly is credited with starting the mythopoetic men's movement in the United States. Until recently, Bly frequently conducted workshops for men with James Hillman, Michael J. Meade, John Lee, and others.

---

13   Frank S. Pittman, *Man Enough: Fathers, Sons, and the Search for Masculinity* (New York: Berkley Publishing Group,1993).

The mythopoetic men's movement is a loose collection of organizations active in men's work since the early 1980s. It was in the public eye in the early 1990s, and the movement now carries on more quietly in the Mankind Project (MKP) and independent psychospiritual practitioners. Mythopoets adopted a general style of psychological self-help inspired by the work of Bly, Robert A. Johnson, Joseph Campbell, and other Jungian authors.

The mythopoetic men's movement spawned a variety of self-help groups and workshops, led by authors such as Bly, John Lee, Michael J. Meade, and Robert L. Moore. The self-help aspect of this movement was portrayed by the popular media as something of a fad, but it continues to this day. Some academic work came from the movement, as well as the creation of various magazines, continuing annual conferences such as the Minnesota Men's Conference and the Great Mother and New Father Conference, and nonprofit organizations such as MKP,[14] which is still active, alive, and well. Mythopoetic practices among women's groups and feminists were more commonly seen as a portion of a more general "women's spirituality."

As a self-help movement, the mythopoetic movement tends not to take explicit stances on political issues such as feminism, gay rights, or family law (such as the issues of divorce, domestic violence, or child custody), preferring instead to stay focused on emotional and psychological well-being.

As part of developing my own work, I've done the MKP's experiential weekend called the New Warrior Training Adventure.[15] Here's how MKP defines the weekend: "The New Warrior Training Adventure is a weekend process of initiation and self-examination that is designed to catalyze the development of a healthy and mature masculine self. It is the hero's journey of classical literature and myth adapted to our modern culture."

The weekend is intended to be a male initiation ritual. MKP states that those who undertake this journey pass through three phases

---

14   http://mankindproject.org/
15   http://mankindproject.org/new-warrior-training-adventure

characteristic of virtually all historic forms of male initiation: descent, ordeal, and return. Participants surrender all electronic devices (cell phones, watches, laptops, etc.), weapons (guns, knives, etc.), and jewelry for the weekend. This is a way of removing the "noise of a man's life," separating the man "from what he is comfortable with," and ensuring the safety of all participants.

Participants must sign a nondisclosure agreement promising not to disclose the specifics of any of the processes used during the weekend to nonparticipants. MKP states that, due to the experiential nature of the program, this policy helps create an experience "uncluttered by expectation" for the next man. Participants must also promise to keep anything they see and hear on the weekend in strict confidence, protecting the privacy of all participants. MKP does, however, encourage participants to freely discuss what they learned about themselves with anyone. I'm not disclosing anything here about the weekend that cannot be found online.

Trainings usually involve thirty to forty participants and some forty to fifty staff members. The course typically takes place at a retreat center over a forty-eight-hour period, with one staff member assigned to each of the participants. Additional staff members provide support for the weekend.

MKP serves an extremely important role in the men's movement, even though there are some unresolved problems within it. For example, the experiential weekend starts off with what felt to me like a heavy dose of patriarchy and control. This is somewhat similar to what initiation has been to men throughout the ages and would be better if it were initiating boys instead of mostly middle-aged men. Although I must say that it does resolve itself by the end of the weekend, I've talked to men who were so turned off or triggered by it that they didn't complete the weekend and realize its benefits, especially men who grew up under the wing of an abusive father. Also, I think MKP mistakes tribalistic ritual for transformation. Author Joseph Gelfer comments that tribal-type rituals may backfire in other cultures, offering this about MKP's approach to initiation and ritual: "Initiation is another theme from which the movement derives its status as spiritual. But again, this is questionable. Initiation is seen as spiritual simply because it is 'tribal,' 'primitive,' and 'ancient' rather than having anything to do with an actual spiritual process. Initiation is just another expedition into [the] fantasy realm."[16]

There's no question that MKP plays an important developmental role in the maturation of men, and I highly recommend the program, especially for young men about to emerge into full manhood. It is incredibly important and necessary work. MKP provides a solid base that the Integral Warrior builds on. I've had many MKP men in the Integral Warrior process who value both, saying that their work with MKP prepared them for the Integral Warrior process and enabled them to go even deeper into their own awareness in their quest for stepping toward the authentic, mature masculine.

The Evangelical Men's Movement

Other examples of contemporary men's work include the evangelical men's movement, typified by the Promise Keepers, a nondenominational group, which is a prime example of the Christian men's movement. Promise Keepers does include therapeutic self-help and emotional intimacy within groups; however, as Frederick Clarkson notes,[17] "Promise Keepers says it aims to create 'men of integrity' while its leaders mouth opportunistic double talk: Honor your wife, but take back your role as head and master of your household. Seek racial 'reconciliation' with hugs and tears among the biblically correct, but ignore racial injustice when it comes to education, jobs and housing."

Because of the scope of this work as a whole, this rather simplistic look at this category also includes the Christian Men's Network, Muscular Christianity, Fellowship of Christian Athletes, and the Catholic Men's Movement. For a more detailed examination of these and other organizations and their patriarchal leanings, I highly recommend Joseph Gelfer's *Numen, Old Men: Contemporary Masculine Spiritualities and the Problem of Patriarchy*.

---

16   Joseph Gelfer, *Numen, Old Men: Contemporary Masculine Spiritualities and the Problem of Patriarchy* (Sheffield, UK: Equinox Publishing, 2009).
17   *Eternal Hostility: The Struggle Between Theocracy and Democracy* (Monroe, ME: Common Courage Press, 1997).

Other Men's Work

There are many groups that fall into the category of "the men's movement," including the profeminist movement, which includes groups like Men Allied Nationally for the Equal Rights Amendment (MAN for the ERA), the National Organization for Men Against Sexism (NOMAS), Rape and Violence End Now (RAVEN) in St. Louis, and Men Overcoming Violence (MOVE) in San Francisco. By the mid-twentieth century, second-wave feminists began to argue that "the personal is political," a trend that legitimized and forced political recognition of women's personal, emotional, and sexual experiences. It also required that profeminist men examine where their personal practices and political ideals connected. By the 1970s, men had begun to examine their own masculinity using a feminist framework.

A couple of other categories enveloped within the men's movement are groups focusing on men's/father's rights, men's liberation, and gay spirituality.[18] I've touched mostly on MKP and Promise Keepers simply because they are the largest men's groups out there. The depth of the men's movement deserves a much deeper look than this book is intended to provide.

Once again, I want to acknowledge and honor my dear friend, community mate, and teacher, Brad Collins, founder of the Shamanic Priest Process[19] for men, with whom I've apprenticed. The Integral Warrior workshop series is partially based on his vision, to which I've added the work I've been doing for several years.

I have intentionally left out philosopher Ken Wilber's *Integral Spirituality*[20] as a part of the men's movement, as its focus, while arguably masculine, is not part of a men's movement and does not deal with intrinsic men's issues. However, in the integral approach championed by Ken, there is a writer connected to the integral movement who does encompass evolutionary masculinity.

---

18   http://gayspirituality.typepad.com/blog/2005/12/mkp_internation. html
19   After Anyaa McAndrew's Shamanic Priestess Process.
20   Ken Wilber, *Integral Spirituality: A Startling New Role for Religion in the Modern and Postmodern World* (Boston: Integral Books, 2006).

Meet David Deida

I've included Deida here because his developmental model of how the masculine and feminine grow through three distinct stages is an important part of the Integral Warrior workshop and because, even though Deida doesn't do men's groups per se, men's groups about his work and philosophies have sprung up organically in a lot of places. When I was living in Seattle in 2007 (population 582,000), I facilitated one of three David Deida–based men's groups there. Imagine my surprise when I moved to Western North Carolina in 2008 and found five or six Deida-based men's groups in Asheville, with a current population of about 75,000!

David Deida's first two published books, *Intimate Communion* (1995) and *It's a Guy Thing* (1997), were oriented to a general readership and introduced some of Deida's key concepts, such as his three-stage model of psychosexual development and an understanding of non–gender-based masculine and feminine identities in a Western cultural context. His three-stage model lays the foundation for a developmental understanding and application of how to move from "first-stage" sexually differentiated codependence and power struggles to "second-stage" sexually neutralized coindependence and cooperation, culminating in the "third-stage" realization of the nondual[21] unity of consciousness and light, with its potentially sexualized expression in love.

> The first stage is characterized by self-serving egotism and also by the traditional 1950s gender roles of man as breadwinner and woman as stay-at-home mom. Stage two is the "fifty-fifty" level of empathy and balance we see in much of the postmodern West today, where equality and congeniality reign supreme between the genders and our main aspiration is really just to get along. Then there's stage three, [Deida] says, where we finally break free of the more timid and passionless aspects of second-stage partnership and begin to reawaken the [non–gender-based] masculine devotion to mission or feminine desire for love that allegedly will bring back our vital core energy and lead to a

---

21   The realization of the oneness of who we are is not some distant goal that only a few can attain.

renewed sense of purposeful being … "There is the [feminine] energetic light aspect of existence, and the [masculine] consciousness aspect of existence, and they are not separate," Deida says. "Light is the shine of consciousness. Consciousness is the cognizance of light or energy. It's the knowing aspect of energy, and it's impossible to separate them. They're together, and that's why sex feels so good, because sex is the recapitulation at the human level of consciousness and light in unity."[22]

In *The Way of the Superior Man* (1997, 2004), Deida summarizes his three-stage view of men's sociocultural evolution in colloquial language: "It is time to evolve beyond the (first-stage) macho jerk ideal, all spine and no heart. It is also time to evolve beyond the (second-stage) sensitive and caring wimp ideal, all heart and no spine. Heart and spine must be united in a single man, and then gone beyond in the fullest expression of love and consciousness possible, which requires a deep relaxation into the infinite openness of this present moment. And this takes a new kind of (third-stage) guts. This is the way of the superior man."[23]

The Way of the Superior Man profoundly changed my life. I had just come off two very quick and intense relationships in which I thought I might have found "the one." While I have a problem with believing in predetermined destiny, it's difficult for me not to believe that both of these women were sent to me so I could learn some very important lessons about both the feminine and the masculine.

Each of these remarkable women touched my soul, and I was inexorably pulled to each, one right after the other. Each, in her own way, was horribly wounded and carried those deep wounds by pushing away and closing down or projecting the causes of those wounds onto men who tried to get too close. In my ignorance at the time, instead of giving them the space they needed, I continued to move forward, driving them even further away. I did not realize at the time how many women have abusive histories. The numbers are staggering, and I wound up in relationships with two, back to back. Reeling from the emotions of what had happened and desperately wanting to understand everyone's role, I

---

22 EnlightenNext, March–May 2009, pp. 58–59.
23 David Deida, (Sounds True, 2006).

began reading everything I could about relationships and why they go wrong. That's when I found Deida's *The Way of the Superior Man*.

Had I not found that book, I might not be doing this work with the masculine today and would surely have never been capable of stepping into the relationship with my beloved Anyaa. Quite simply, she would have eaten me alive! One of the extraordinary things I learned through reading Deida was how to "open" my beloved without being wimpy or letting go of the polarity that is so needed between the masculine and the feminine. This is the third-stage quality of being able to open my heart without giving up my masculine essence—without going soft or being so much in my feminine that I lose the ability to penetrate the heart of my beloved. At the same time, I retain the ability to move between the masculine and feminine poles as needed in whatever moment arises, always with the intention of keeping the polarity, the tension between the opposites, active and alive, always passionate, always connected, always with the intention of giving the greatest gift the masculine can give the feminine: the ability to relax.

Deida's work is a huge step in the right direction, for both men and women, and yet there seem to be other places to eventually go, beyond third stage, into the purity of the sacred union of the Sacred Masculine and the Divine Feminine—a place where both feminine and masculine just seem to drop away into oneness.

There are critics[24] who think that Deida's work ultimately feels unsustainable and simplistic, especially over time. For them, the focus of Deida's work seems weighted toward sex, but this also feels reductionistic because Deida emphasizes that sex is not the whole answer; it's just part of the path to the love and intimacy we seek.

Sex—as Deida points out through Michaela Boehm, the only counselor in the world personally trained and authorized by David Deida—is where most of our contractions show up, and that is the place where there can be the most openings around the contractions that keep us unconscious. I couldn't agree more.

---

24   Joseph Gelfer, *Numen, Old Men: Contemporary Masculine Spiritualities and the Problem of Patriarchy*, 2009.

In the fall of 2011, I attended a David Deida workshop weekend at the Omega Institute in New York called the Sexual Body and Yoga of Light workshop. In the experiential practices, I felt a certain reductionistic simplicity where the masculine was broken down into pure presence and the feminine was broken down into pure sexuality. I won't go into the details of the practice, but the exercise was ultimately unsatisfying for me (not that I didn't have an exquisite partner who played her role perfectly) because it felt incomplete and partial. It was just one exercise, and exercises are, by their very nature, somewhat reductionistic. After all, they're just exercises, not real life. The triggers around an exercise may be signs of the things we need to work on, but the time to really pay attention to what triggers us is in our real-life experiences, especially around sex and relationship. Nothing pushes our buttons like relationship. The weekend was delicious. Deida is a wonderful facilitator and has an amazing presence. He is one of the best I've seen at cutting through the bullshit we each bring to the stories we tell about ourselves. If you have an opportunity to attend one of his workshops, go.

Deida's approach to sex, relationship, and enlightenment is subtle, complex, multilayered, and multifaceted,[25] and it is perfect for a postmodern world of people who are desperately seeking more depth and understanding of who they are and how it all fits together. Because of the complexity of his work, he is often misunderstood and often misinterpreted. For instance, he is seemingly mired in controversy, drawing criticism around what some see as his political stance, with some mistakenly alleging an element of misogyny. Deida suggests there are only two ways to deal with women and the world: "Either renounce sexuality and the 'seemingly constant demands of woman and the world' or fuck both to smithereens, to ravish them with your love unsheathed."[26] Deida is also accused of holding little sympathy with "no means no" campaigns[27]: Deida says "What she wants is not what she says."[28] What Deida is talking about is the play that happens in the

---

25   EnlightenNext, March-May 2009, pp. 58–59
26   Joseph Gelfer, *Numen, Old Men: Contemporary Masculine Spiritualities and the Problem of Patriarchy,* 2009, p. 121.
27   http://numenoldmen.wordpress.com/tag/david-deida/
28   http://www.bluetruth.org/index.php/What_She_Wants_Is_Not_What_She_Says

bedroom between consenting adults, not what happens in the workplace or other public places. Again, it's very easy to misinterpret what Deida is talking about, especially if you are still hung up on your own shadows. I did not find him misogynistic in his workshop, and these are complex matters, easily mistaken for what sometimes can appear as a lack of political correctness. Last, even Deida himself has characterized his recent work more as "spiritual theater" rather than "religious teaching."[29] If that's the case, I have to say that it's really good theater.

Okay. I have a problem with most teachers. You might even consider me "guru-phobic" (I certainly do), but like Wilber, I take the position that everyone has "a piece of the truth," and as a self-proclaimed synthesizer of multiple wisdoms, I take the good stuff from everything and leave the rest behind. Deida's got a lot of truth, and his three-stage view of masculine and feminine development is simply the best out there for Western culture. That said, I expect you, dear reader, to approach everything I say in the same manner. Deida does a great job of summarizing what the new masculine looks like, and I use it in my work with the Integral Warrior.

Deida's model is key to understanding how the masculine (and feminine) grows; as with Spiral Dynamics, a values-based system of development featured in a later chapter, the shift to later-stage consciousness is enhanced with an understanding of how and why people change.

The New Masculine

What does this "new masculine" look like? What are the qualities that define the new masculine, and how is it different from the old masculine?

The masculine, directional and focused, is defined and guided by the search for *freedom*, like a jungle guide with a machete cutting through anything that gets in his way. But not everyone uses masculine energy to search for that freedom in the same way. The feminine path, on the other hand, is about the search for love, or communion.

---

29   *David Deida: The Complete Recordings*, Volumes 1–4 (Audio CD).

How a man seeks freedom depends on his particular needs, and those needs typically change in three stages:

- **First-stage** needs are about gaining something, like food, money, sex, power, or fame. A first-stage man tends to form a dependent relationship with his woman. First-stage masculine (and feminine) characterizes the vast majority of men in Western culture. For most of us, it's what our parents' marriages looked like: the man goes off to work to earn a living to support his woman and family, while his wife stays home, cleaning and raising children, looking sadly like a woman in a fifties ad for a stove, cooking in a dress, high heels, and an apron. He's in charge, and he finds his freedom by getting *more* of everything. Today's economics have had a profound impact on that image, but for most couples, it's still the man who's in charge.

- **Second-stage** needs are about self-improvement, authenticity, being in touch with your inner wisdom, and creating a Garden of Eden on earth. A second-stage man is interested in forming an equal partnership with his woman, what Deida calls a "50/50 relationship." This is where women began integrating their inner masculine (as a result of feminism) and, as a response, men began integrating their inner feminine, largely at the expense of denying their own masculine or feminine. Here, the search for a man's freedom is characterized not by *more* but by *better.*

- **Third-stage** needs are about letting go of self-definition, relaxing the endless search for completion, feeling through the tension of this present moment, and surrendering limits on openness as each moment arises and dissolves in love. A third-stage man enjoys a relationship with his partner based on the practice of intimate communion. A third-stage man has reintegrated his masculine and no longer *seeks* freedom but *becomes* freedom by embodying it in his very being. This is the Divine Masculine. Likewise, the feminine is no longer looking for love but *becomes* love.[30]

---

30 Adapted from David Deida

The man who ascribes to the new masculine finds his freedom from within and is not concerned with external causation. He may have things, but he doesn't find his self-worth or his freedom in them. He finds his freedom in the present moment by surrendering into that moment and letting go of self-definition. The new masculine no longer searches for freedom; he embodies freedom itself, always transcending, always including that which arises spontaneously in every moment.

A man who embodies the new masculine no longer depends on someone else's opinion of him, although he can easily relax into a deep listening state when someone offers counsel. It means being able to hold space for family, friends, a partner, and the world. It means being in service to the world without negating his own needs in a codependent way. It means sometimes saying no in a loving and compassionate way. It means living at his edge, always pushing himself to be on purpose, and giving his unique gifts to the world, whatever they might be. It means challenging other men, and himself, to give up the things that limit surrender into gifting.

It means having his mission and his purpose aligned with his life, filling his core, and having a deep spiritual awareness, not dogmatic drivel. The new masculine penetrates the world to magnify an open heart, love, and depth—again, his gift to the world.

The third-stage masculine has some unique characteristics that don't exist at the earlier stages. Moving into the third stage means being able to move freely, at will, between masculine and feminine qualities that serve the perfect moment that continuously arises in the fullness of love and nonseparation.

Once men and women have fully integrated their masculine and feminine sides, they are able to move back and forth between the two at will when either is needed in a given situation. This ability allows the feminine to open fully and the masculine to become the essence of freedom *and* love—both in the same person, regardless of gender. Therein lies the possibility of sacred union and higher purpose for the good of all beings and is the ultimate expression of *be*-ing.

This is the purpose that drives the Integral Warrior process: to help men prepare for, or to move to, the emerging new masculine, the next step in masculine evolutionary spirituality, or what David Deida calls third-stage masculinity.

Ironically, it seems to me that the men's movement, in its varied forms, has been shocked into existence by highly visible patriarchal behavior and masculine aspects adopted by some women—particularly in powerful women or women in business—the return of the Goddess and women claiming their own inner masculine; cultural, political, and economic circumstances; and our rising need to reclaim, rediscover, and reinvent what it means to be a "man," and not what it means only from the feminine perspective.

The biggest problem with women integrating the masculine is that the only model of the masculine they've been offered is the patriarchal version. This is not their fault, although they must take some responsibility for it. We need the new masculine to model what it means to be a conscious man partly so that women can integrate the healthiest version of the masculine into their own being.

Many women today are crying out for the Divine Masculine to show up and enter sacred marriage with the Divine Feminine, both in external and internal realms, in the individual and the collective.

There is no doubt that men are playing catch up with the work women have been doing. We have surrendered to a hero image that we can't possibly attain and the accumulation of wealth, disregarding everything but our own ego and power. Patriarchy is the consciousness of greed, the conqueror, and moves forward willfully, throwing its weight around and bending all before it to its will. The patriarchy is the bully ... and worse. Patriarchy is the enemy of the healthy masculine.

As men, "we are the product of all that has come before us: the Mesolithic hunters, gatherers and Neolithic farmers of matrilineal culture (7000–2000 BC); the Indo-European warriors emphasizing the male sky gods in the centuries of the Bronze and Iron Age (2000–800 BC); the turn of the millennium with the advent of Christian mythology and its concepts of dualistic division between body and soul, world and spirit and Original Sin; and finally the age of scientific rationalism that allows for nothing supernatural or spiritual and reduces the universe to a language of numerical abstraction—mathematics."[31]

We are also the wounded warriors.

Centuries of patriarchy have numbed our souls, our feelings, and our spirit, and we are beginning to awaken to the need to love and work in ways that heal our lives, the lives of those we love and the lives of those we want to love and want to be worthy of.

With later-stage consciousness comes new awareness about the changing role of the masculine. The new masculine, this Divine Masculine— Eros—considers all other aspects, integrating and calling as many perspectives into a man's *be*-ing as he can maintain with fierce awareness, stretching the boundaries of what is possible while bravely holding space for the feminine, nature, body, spirit, integrity, authenticity, wisdom, and heart. The new masculine man moves forward, aligning with his true purpose and the full embodiment of presence for the highest good of all beings.

Opening Is a Conscious Choice

In the deepest relationship I've ever been in my life, I continue to be challenged—to stretch, to step up, to be bigger than I've ever been, to be fully present with my beloved and the world. I'm in this relationship because I'm finally at a place where my consciousness can fearlessly hold it, embrace it, and fully open to it as my heart explodes in radiance and gratitude.

In the end, we—you and I, the men who choose to make this conscious journey—are the ones who will ultimately decide what the new masculine will look like, and it won't be one model. It will take a myriad of forms, of essences, of individuation and integration, sculpted into as many different images as there are men who choose to embody it.

I invite you to step into the Divine Masculine, the Integral Warrior.

---

31   K. C. Holt, "Images of the Divine Masculine," 2006, http://www. widdershins.org/vol2iss6/y9610.htm

Chapter 2:   How the Masculine Grows

As we learned in the first chapter, the masculine is directional and focused and is defined and guided by the search for freedom, cutting through any and all obstacles in his path. We also learned that not everyone uses masculine energy to search for that freedom in the same way. The essential style in which the masculine searches for freedom is the way of the warrior, or as Joseph Campbell calls it, the hero's journey. But the way of the warrior is not an easy path: "It is by going down into the abyss that we recover the treasures of life," Campbell says. "Where you stumble, there lies your treasure."

Whether a man's developmental center of gravity is in the first or second stage, if he stays awake, continues to grow, and doesn't stagnate or become captive to the trappings of his current stage of development, he will eventually experience a "dark night of the soul."

Some think change can happen through all light and love. I remember that several years ago I thought my consciousness was sufficiently developed and that I could finally evolve and grow consciously and smoothly, as opposed to the way we mostly seem to grow—through pain. I hadn't yet stepped into a truly conscious relationship, and I hadn't discovered the Shamanic Breathwork Process.[32] It appears that contact with deep and hidden elements of our subconscious being, or

---

32   See Chapter 8.

the "abyss," as Campbell so eloquently puts it, is an essential part of any evolutionary growth process.

Ken Wilber, in the foreword to Andrew Cohen's book *Living Enlightenment,*[33] puts it this way:

> So, can you stand the heat? Or would you like more soft and consoling words of comfort, more consolation prizes for an Enlightenment that will continue to elude you? Would you like a pat on the back, or are you ready to be skinned and fried? May I suggest this? If you can stand the heat, you will indeed come to realize that your true glory lies where you cease to exist, where the self-contraction has uncoiled in the vast expanse of all space, where your separate self has been roasted and replaced by infinity resplendent—a radical release much too obvious to see, much too simple to believe, much too near to be attained—and your real Self will quietly but surely announce its Presence as it calmly embraces the entire universe and swallows galaxies whole.

One of the ways men (and women) step into the abyss is through relationship. Nothing brings your stuff up like relationship—family, work, your partner, but *especially* your partner. If you're willing and able, a relationship is a testing ground to see just how evolved you are. Being in relationship is a *practice,* and practice you must if the relationship is to succeed or not go flat, and the proof of your embodied realization is going to be in your relationships, especially the one with your partner. Relationship will bring up every childhood wound you ever incurred, and we've all got them. Relationship, one of many paths to transformation, is, in my opinion, the simplest, most available, most immediate path to transformation and transcendent experience we can take. It's the most life changing, here-it-is-folks, nondual, ordinary path to spiritual realization, and really paying attention to what's going on in your relationship can put you on the fast track to Spirit.

So the first-stage man finds himself no longer satisfied by his acquisitional consciousness—a better car, a bigger house, the corner office or the

---

33   Lenox, MA: Moksha Press, 2002.

perfect job, a trophy wife, or money and power. The first-stage man's goal is outside his body, outside the moment, and he is going to get it. Victory for a first-stage man is all about getting what he wants—the car, the cash, the country, whatever there is to get. However, once he gets what he wanted, he sometimes finds that he's still not satisfied and realizes that he is standing at the abyss of incompleteness. Cognitive dissonance sets in, but a first-stage man with a pathological bent just tries to get more, thinking that will solve the dark night of the soul, the dissatisfaction, and the incompleteness he's feeling.

Some first-stage men come to the realization that the definition of insanity, as we've all heard, is continuing to do what we've always done and expecting different results. These men, experiencing an uncomfortable tension or cognitive dissonance in their lives, begin to seek their freedom by *changing* their behavior instead of justifying it.

This behavior change moves men away from the strong first-stage acquisitional approach and leads them inward to conquer, not the world, but their own inner limitations. A man in this place is not looking to get more of something; he wants to improve who he is and become a "better" man. He may practice meditation, martial arts, or psychotherapy; travel to experience other cultures; and generally try to soften his edges. Men often start this second stage by beginning to integrate their feminine sides. This makes perfect sense, actually, as second-stage women must go through the process of integrating their masculine and begin to look and act a lot like first-stage men, the only model of the masculine most women have ever come in contact with. It is also part of the evolutionary process for both the masculine and the feminine, as they each integrate their opposites, or what I call "oppositional integration." This oppositional integration of the masculine and the feminine, with women and men, respectively, is a critical part of our maturation process and our spiritual evolution.

The problem that arises with this oppositional integration is that it often comes with an unconscious rejection of our native aspect. That is, men, in integrating the feminine, tend to unconsciously reject their native masculine aspect, and women, in integrating the masculine, tend to unconsciously reject their native feminine aspect. Again, this is a necessary step in the evolution of the masculine and feminine, but it's certainly not the endgame.

The oppositional integration can create another challenge—the polarity between the masculine and feminine sometimes goes away. If we think of polarity in terms of a magnet, with polarized poles, we find that when we maintain polarity, the magnets are unmistakably drawn to each other. Change one of the poles, however, and the magnets push each other away. This analogy applies to our sexual relationships. When our native aspects meet in the middle, we tend to become best friends, but the sexual quality of our relationship tends to flatten out. In order to maintain sexual polarity, one partner has to hold the masculine and one has to hold the feminine, and it really doesn't matter which. It is my belief that in any intimate relationship, there are masculine and feminine roles—someone who is more in their masculine and someone who is more in their feminine at any point in time. A couple could switch masculine and feminine roles and maintain polarity, but if only one switches, they're probably going to watch a movie instead of having an intimate evening. It doesn't mean they're not going to have a good time.

I have a friend who doesn't get the importance of sexual polarity in his relationship. He loves that he and his significant other are in a balanced relationship, each holding equal parts of the masculine and feminine. They are great friends but not intimate. It's definitely safe, but it is certainly not passionate. They are great roommates.

I sometimes wonder if they had passion when they met. Was it polarity that attracted them in the beginning? In my own relationship, my wife and I are very aware of when one or the other is in a particular essence, and if we're both strongly in our masculine and directional, we know we're probably going to butt heads. If we're both in our feminine, we can be great friends, but as she feels me drop the polarity, it's fairly clear that passion is not in play.

Having not reintegrated his masculine after integrating the feminine is going to ultimately leave a man feeling unsatisfied. Some men at this stage start to feel that dissatisfaction, that emptiness, that incompleteness, and they once again begin to search for a cure for their cognitive dissonance.

He thinks, *I've done everything I was supposed to do. Why am I still not happy?* The reason he's not fulfilled is that he is still trapped by his own fears, attached to his fear of death and the dread of separation.

Cognitive dissonance is most powerful when it is about our self-image. Feelings of foolishness, immorality, and so on (including internal projections during decision making) are dissonance in action. Dissonance increases with the importance and impact of the decision, along with the difficulty of reversing it.[34] This drives us to seek change, and so we set out on the hero's journey once again.

As I've already described third-stage masculine in Chapter 1, let me repeat the very brief description of it here: Third-stage needs are about letting go of self-definition, relaxing the endless search for completion, feeling through the tension of this present moment, and surrendering limits on openness as each moment arises and dissolves in love. A third-stage man enjoys a relationship with his partner based on the practice of intimate communion. A third-stage man has reintegrated his masculine and no longer *seeks* freedom but *becomes* freedom by embodying it in his very being. This is the Divine Masculine.

I'm not so foolish or caught up in my ego to believe that I live at third stage or that I embody third-stage capacities. I do believe that I have third-stage moments—as well as first-stage and second-stage moments. Sometimes I behave in the acquisitional manner of first-stage masculine, and sometimes I'm in my feminine, solidly in second stage. Sometimes I do this on purpose because it's required in the moment, and sometimes I do it without thinking, acting unawakened. What can I say? I know my wife sometimes thinks I'm the reincarnation of a 1940s consciousness. They may be out there, but I don't know anyone who embodies third-stage masculine all the time. I also know I'm getting better at it. My wife also says that I embody the new masculine better than anyone she knows. I'm not sure about that, but I know I've found my passion and my purpose and that I'm on fire about it. I also know I can stand in the fire of the strongest feminine and not take it personally—most of the time. Third-stage masculine is an emergent quality, and maybe fifty or

---

34   http://changingminds.org/explanations/theories/cognitive_dissonance.htm

a hundred years from now, people will look back and think how foolish and undeveloped we were. Or maybe they'll look back and thank us for standing just past the leading edge of today's consciousness, paving the way for their more awakened qualities and capacities.

Awakening the new masculine is about that hero's journey—preparation for the eventual and, hopefully, inevitable emergence of the third-stage masculine.

Where Are the Models for the New Masculine?

I'm often asked by men who want to shift their perspectives on their own masculinity who the models are for the new masculine. It's a great question.

Ken Wilber and Andrew Cohen address the question in "What It Means to Be a Man: Redefining the Masculine Principle at the Leading Edge of Cultural Evolution."[35] In that discussion, Cohen says that in researching the article, it was "very hard to get men, even those who seem to be very sophisticated in their cognitive capacity, to express some example of what they thought an evolved man would look like."

I agree with him that, because of postmodernism's feminization of the masculine (second-stage masculine), there is a cultural block and fear around stepping up and embracing the greater potentials of the masculine. One of those problems, from my perspective, is that third-stage masculine looks a lot like first-stage masculine from the vantage point of second-stage masculine. Wilber points out that postmodernism prevents us from using wisdom judgment (discernment) and discrimination around our inherent capacities, in this case, our masculine essence. As second-stage men, we have worked so hard to suppress our masculinity that we have a difficult time seeing the positive aspects of that masculinity.

Some argue that both the masculine and the feminine should drop away into a state of oneness, the nondual or enlightenment, but before that can happen, we have to do the work that heals our wounded masculine

---

35 *EnlightenNext* Magazine, Issue 41, October 2008, p. 36.

and feminine selves or we can't get to that enlightened place. Of course, there are those rare individuals who can embody the nondual without having to reintegrate their inner essences or who seem to heal them outright from some sort of spiritual enlightenment, but most of us have to work at it. The danger of not doing the work for the majority of us is that we skip the developmental stages required to fully integrate, and we wind up in spiritual bypass: all light, no darkness.

And it should be obvious to all that the light cannot exist without the darkness.

So, let's come back to the original question: "Who are the models for the new masculine?" The very same question could be asked of the feminine, which, at second stage, is at least in the process of integrating the inner masculine and at third stage is beginning to reintegrate the feminine. This issue will be addressed in another book planned for the future.

In an evolutionary sense, this is all new territory, and *we*—the men and women who are doing this work, as teachers *and* students, happening at the leading edge of consciousness—are the ones who will determine what this evolutionary shift looks like. As we step into this work, willingly and consciously, *we* become the models for the new masculine.

The new masculine lives his deepest realization. My sense is that most men simply have no idea what this means. Upon an initial examination, it's easy to confuse it with one's purpose, or mission, but it's actually much more simple than that: A man's deepest realization comes about simply by being totally present in the moment … and this moment … and this moment. Who are you when you connect to being fully present in each moment? What is your essence at that point when you let go of creating your story about yesterday, which no longer exists except as a memory, and tomorrow, which simply doesn't exist at all except as an expectation or a desire?

For me, it's not about being perfect at one thing—it's about being present at whatever I'm doing and connecting to my source, whether I'm doing dishes, cleaning, being with my wife, working at my purpose, or doing nothing at all. It's not about being enlightened, for to seek enlightenment would rob me of my freedom. When I'm present in the moment, it's as if the moment is luminous, and I am the witness to all that arises in that moment.

So how does a man do this? How do I do this? It's based on my meditation practices of several years of sitting and then having the realization that *every moment is a meditation practice,* an awareness of nonseparation, a unity consciousness, and no longer feeling the need to sit but to just be. It also means living without fear, knowing there's a bigger picture over which I know I have no control, surrendering into the moment and letting go of everything else.

It doesn't mean that I'm not triggered or that I don't plan for tomorrow, think about yesterday, hurt, cry, laugh. It means I try to do it all consciously, recognizing everything, and that I'm not tied to it. It's flexibility, it's flow, and it's freedom. It's art … and it's love. So stop reading this, take a deep breath, and relax into the present moment. There is nothing else.

Ah … *sweet freedom.*

Figure 1 shows what each of these stages looks like in four different developmental planes, or lines: physical, mental, emotional, and spiritual. Spend some time noticing what each of the three stages looks like in comparison to the others and how the shift to the next stage affects the worldview and responds to the previous stage. Then, take some time and think about where you fit in.

Three Stages of the Masculine

Developmental Line	First Stage Traditional Masculinity	Second Stage Feminized Masculinity	Third Stage Integrated Masculinity
Physical	Hard	Soft	Flexible
	Dominating	Submissive	Capable
	Tough	Gentle	Strong
	Soldier	Pacifist	Warrior
	Killer	Gatherer	Hunter
	Coercive	Pliant	Firm
	Controlling	Controlled	Vigilant
	Lord and Master	Consort	Partner
	Destructive	Immobile	Generative
Emotional	Closed	Unprotected	Receptive
	Numb	Flooded	Feeling
	Codependent	Dependent	Interdependent
	Demanding	Smothering	Nurturing
	Aggressive	Passive	Assertive
	Cynical	Naïve	Fresh/Humorous
	Sex Partner	Pleaser	Lover
	Defensive	Wounded	Deep Feeling
	Repressed	Contained	Wild/Playful
	Bastard	Nice Guy	Fierce
Mental/Cognitive	Compartmentalized	Merged	Eclectic/Individuated
	Penetrating	Diffused	Insightful
	Analytical	Synthetic	Discriminating
	Splitting	Joining	Holds Paradox
	Linear	Circular	Holonomic
	Dominating		
	Hierarchy	Anarchy	Community
	Exploitive	Conservative	Resourceful
	Rules and Laws	Procedures	Personal Ethics
	Doctor	Magical Thinker	Healer
Spiritual	Patriarchal	Matriarchal	Polytheistic
	Absolutist	Dualistic	Paradoxical

Uninitiated	Seeker	Initiated
Immobile	Flighty	Grounded
Contracted Self	Selfless	Expanded Self
Divided	Disassociated	Embodied
Dogma	Belief	Direct Experience
Exclusive	Inclusive	Selective
Priest	Guru	Mentor/Elder

Figure 1: Three Stages of the Masculine – Adapted from Aaron Kipnis, *Knights without Armor*

CHAPTER 3:   SHIFTING PERSPECTIVES
INTO LATER-STAGE CONSCIOUSNESS

We are awaiting the new global founding Fathers and Mothers who will frame an integral system of governance that will call us to our more encompassing future, that will act as a gentle pacer of transformation for the entire spiral of human development, honoring each and every wave as it unfolds, yet kindly inviting each and all to even greater depth. —Ken Wilber, *A Theory of Everything*[36]

THIS CHAPTER AND THE next one, on developmental models, are extremely important to the Integral Warrior process and awakening the new masculine. I present these as models of how and why we change because I believe that once we understand the mechanics and processes of change, it's easier for us to actually effect the change we want to see in ourselves and in the world. In addition, understanding these models gives us a common language that allows us to talk about the process of awakening in a much deeper context.

Moving into later-stage consciousness requires the ability to see, experience, and assume as many perspectives as possible. In fact, this ability to hold multiple perspectives, even when they are seemingly opposed to one another—or paradoxical—is one of the hallmarks of the

---

36   Ken Wilber, *A Theory of Everything: An Integral Vision for Business, Politics, Science and Spirituality*. Shambhala Publications, 2000, p. 90.

Integral Warrior. Being multiperspectival is also key to understanding why so many people seem so irrationally diametrically opposed to each other. One of the ways to develop the ability to hold differing perspectives is to expand our understanding on why people have differing opinions on so many subjects. Integral, or integral theory, helps explain why.

Simply put, integral, and integral theory, is the most comprehensive map of human consciousness ever developed. Integral is also a dynamic, new worldview that appears to have burst onto the global stage. Called the integral worldview by many, it is a "meta-paradigm of reality, a unifying cultural consciousness that both underlies and conditions an individual's way of knowing, seeing and acting in the world."[37] In other words, we're able to see, honor, and understand an opposing worldview because we recognize that there is an element of truth in it, no matter how far-fetched it might seem.

Historically, new worldviews emerge only when the previous worldviews can no longer solve the new problems that arise. When a new worldview emerges, it is a response to the Albert Einstein quote, "We can't solve problems by using the same kind of thinking we used when we created them." Ironically, each new emerging worldview is also more complex than the previous one, which then creates an entirely new set of problems … so far.

Many developmental systems recognize that new worldviews have emerged only a handful of times in our history and that, in the order of their emergence, they are archaic, magic, mythic, modern, and postmodern.

Another definition of *integral* says,

> The integral approach offers a comprehensive, multidimensional philosophy as well as a set of tools with broad applications, from an academic structure of analysis to a framework for vital personal practices. The integral approach unifies East and West, past and present, and helps inject meaning into existence, with its focus on Spirituality and human development. Presently,

---

37   Lawrence Wollersheim, Executive Director of Integrative Spirituality (now called Universe Spirit), http://universespirit.org/cms/

there are a number of global initiatives that are formulating a "big picture" of the extensive knowledge presently available to humanity, from the traditional to the innovative. This "big picture" strives to bring together all voices and traditions to craft a vision for both problem solving and enlightened living.[38]

I soon put a description of integral theory into my own words: "Integral is a comprehensive and inclusive philosophy, and on a deeper level, an emerging consciousness; a grand synthesis uniting eastern and western philosophy, religion, science, politics, art, morals, values, meaning, that can apply to any contemporary issue. It's a new way of looking at the world, its problems, and their possible solutions."

No discussion of integral would be—well, integral—without talking about Wilber, the world's leading "integral" philosopher.[39] Wilber is the most widely translated academic writer in America, with twenty-five books translated into some thirty foreign languages, and is the first philosopher-psychologist to have his collected works published while still alive. Wilber is an internationally acknowledged leader and the preeminent scholar of the Integral stage of human development, which continues to gather momentum around the world. His many books, all of which are still in print, can be found at Amazon.com. Some of his more popular books include *Integral Spirituality*; *No Boundary*; *Grace and Grit*; and *Sex, Ecology, Spirituality*, as well as the "everything" books: *A Brief History of Everything* (one of his best-selling books) and *A Theory of Everything*, which is probably the shortest introduction to his work. Wilber is the founder of Integral Institute, Inc.; the cofounder of Integral Life, Inc.; and a senior fellow of Integral Life Spiritual Center.

Wilber has been called the "Einstein of consciousness" and has written over twenty-five books exploring different facets of human development and cultural evolution. It's more than fair to say that "discovering" Wilber drastically changed my life, and if you are not already familiar with his work, I urge you to find out more about him and his writing.

---

38 from Matrix Integral, an organization that no longer exists that was devoted to supporting integral education initiatives around the world.
39 http://www.enlightennext.org/magazine/bios/ken-wilber.asp

One of the first things people start asking themselves after reading a couple of Wilber's books is, "Now that I have this growing knowledge, what do I do with it?" I've also heard time and time again from others, "If you deeply understand this stuff, there's no going back." It's like you've been running on a depleted oxygen source, and all of a sudden you can breathe this pure, fresh oxygen. How *could* you go back?

Wilber says that all of the wisdom traditions have a core of truth running through them and that the key is to find a means of putting these truths together in a useful way. As Wilber started "mapping" the essential ideas from various sources, he hit upon the key idea that has organically grown in his writings into something called the "AQAL model" (short for "all quadrants, levels, lines, states, and types"). We will look at this next.

AQAL: "All Quadrants, All Levels"

AQAL (pronounced *ah-qwul*) represents the core of Wilber's work. AQAL stands for "all quadrants, all levels," but it equally connotes "all lines," "all states," and "all types." These are the five irreducible categories of Wilber's model of manifest existence. In order for an account of the cosmos to be complete, Wilber believes that it must include each of these five categories, or what Wilber calls the Five Aspects. For Wilber, only such an account can be accurately called "integral." In the essay, "Excerpt C: The Ways We Are in This Together," Wilber describes AQAL as "one suggested architecture of the Kosmos."[40]

All of Wilber's AQAL categories—quadrants, lines, levels, states, and types—relate to relative truth in the two-truths doctrine of Buddhism,[41] to which he subscribes. According to Wilber, none of them are true in an absolute sense: only formless awareness, "the simple feeling of being," exists absolutely.

An account or theory is said to be AQAL, and thus integral (inclusive

---

40   http://wilber.shambhala.com/html/books/kosmos/excerptC/intro-1. cfm

41   John B. Buescher, *Echoes from an Empty Sky: The Origins of the Two Truths* (Ithaca, NY: Snow Lion Publications, 2005).

or comprehensive), if it accounts for, or makes reference to, all four quadrants and four major levels in Wilber's ontological scheme, described below. The AQAL system has been critiqued for not taking into account the lack of change in the biological structure of the brain at the human level (complex neocortex), this role being taken instead by human-made artifacts.[42]

According to integral theory, there are at least four primary dimensions or perspectives (all quadrants, Figure 2) through which we can experience the world: subjective, intersubjective, objective, and interobjective. These four perspectives, represented graphically, are the upper-left, lower-left, upper-right, and lower-right quadrants.

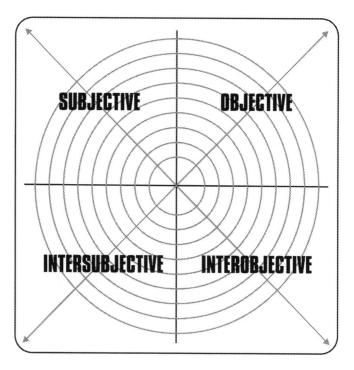

Figure 2

---

42   Steve McIntosh, *Integral Consciousness and the Future of Evolution* (St. Paul, MN: Paragon House, 2007).

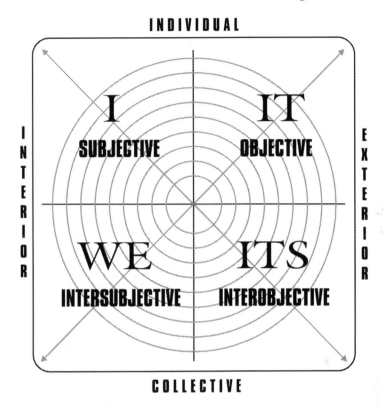

Figure 3

In the subjective—or upper-left—quadrant (see Figures 3 and 4), we find the world of our individual, interior experiences: our thoughts, emotions, memories, states of mind, perceptions, and immediate sensations—in other words, our "I" space.

In the intersubjective—or lower-left—quadrant, we find the world of our collective, interior experiences: our shared values, meanings, language, relationships, and cultural background—in other words, our "we" space.

In the objective—or upper-right—quadrant, we find the world of individual, exterior things: our material bodies (including the brain) and anything that we can see or touch (or observe scientifically) in time and space—in other words, our "it" space.

In the interobjective—or lower-right—quadrant, we find the world of collective, exterior things: systems, networks, technology, government, and the natural environment—in other words, our "its" space.

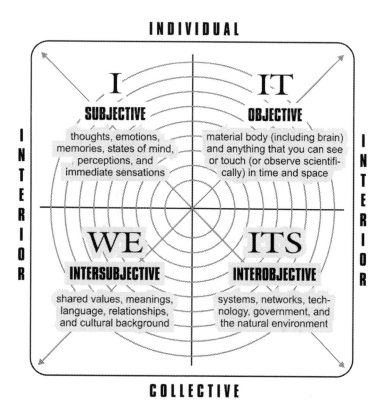

Figure 4

What's the point of looking at the world through a four-quadrant lens?

The simple answer is that anything less is narrow, partial, and fragmented. Integral theory maintains that all four quadrants must be considered and that all are important. So, for example, to respond to the question of what is more real, the brain (with its neural pathways and structures) or the mind (with its thoughts and perceptions), integral theory answers, *Both.*

Moreover, we add that the mind and the brain are situated in cultural and systemic contexts that influence both inner experience and brain activity in irreducible ways.

What's more important in human behavior—the psychology of the mind (upper left) or the cultural conditioning of the individual (lower left)? Integral theory answers, again, *both*. What is more critical in social development—the habits, customs, and norms of a culture (lower left), or the products it produces (like guns and steel—lower right)? Integral theory answers, *Both*.

All four quadrants are real, all are important, and all are essential for understanding your world.

While some might like to reduce reality to the mind (upper-left quadrant), others to the brain (upper-right quadrant), still others to the influence of cultural context (lower-left quadrant), and yet others to the effect of systems ("It's the economy, stupid!" i.e., lower-right quadrant), integral theory holds that *all four quadrants* are indispensable. The more we can consciously include the four quadrants in our perspectives, the more whole, balanced, healthy, comprehensive, and effective our actions will be.

And it all boils down to just four dimensions. It's as easy as I, we, it, and its![43]

---

43   Graphics and text used with permission from Ken Wilber.

Masculine Power
in the Integral Model

INDIVIDUAL

Upper Left Quadrant **Mental Power** Managing your inner state and emotions Analytical/Logistical assessment Creativity Awareness Focus	**Upper Right Quadrant** **Physical Power** Physical health Strength Agility Speed Martial power
Lower Left Quadrant **Social Power** Creating and maintaining relationships Interpersonal skills Care for others	**Lower Right Quadrant** **Structural Power** Your position in society Your occupation Which systems you use How you get things done

INTERIOR — EXTERIOR

COLLECTIVE

Figure 5

The Five Aspects

We've just taken a brief and fairly simple journey through the four quadrants of the integral model, which are considered to be four fundamental dimensions of existence. However, no examination of the integral model would be complete without taking a brief journey into what is called the "five aspects" of that model. As explained at the beginning of this chapter, that model, including the four quadrants, is sometimes referred to as the "AQAL" model.

Very briefly, the five aspects are:

- **Quadrants**: The inside and outside view of the individual and the collective, as well as the collective and individual view of the inside and outside.

- **Levels** (or stages): Natural emergent qualities that unfold in increasing complexity; for example, egocentric, ethnocentric, worldcentric.

- **Lines:** I'm good at some things, not so good at others. These also have developmental aspects.

- **States:** Temporary experiences like waking, sleeping, dreaming, as well as altered-state experiences like meditation.

- **Types:** Masculine, Feminine, Myers Briggs, Enneagram, astrology signs

The AQAL map shows how all of these aspects fit together in a map of human consciousness, and we've already examined the four quadrants. Let's touch on each of the other four.

Levels: One has to go through the lower (earlier) levels, also known as stages, before going through the higher (later) levels because the higher levels are constituted by the lower-level components. When represented graphically, the levels should appear as concentric circles (see Figure 6) with higher levels transcending *but also including* lower ones. One of the best models we use in the Integral Warrior is Spiral Dynamics. Some people object to the hierarchal concept of levels but fail to distinguish between dominator and natural hierarchies.

Lines: We all have multiple lines of development, which are sometimes referred to as intelligences. Some, not all, of these lines are cognitive, moral, aesthetic, spiritual, self-identifying, psychosexual, and interpersonal. Any of us can be highly developed in one or more lines and not in others. However, Wilber also says that we cannot be highly morally developed without the prerequisite cognitive development. An integral psychograph is used to look at our strengths and weaknesses around our lines of development.

States: *States* refers to aspects of consciousness that are temporal, passing, experiential, and phenomenal. Anyone at any level can have a "peak experience" of a higher level without being able to embody it. Thus, primitive shamans were able to get a taste of the "nondual," but the experience was always interpreted at their own level of understanding. State experiences in the Integral Warrior process include induced states—like shamanic journeying, Shamanic Breathwork, guided meditations, gestalt therapy, Insight Dialogue, and tonglen meditation—and spontaneous or peak states in sudden shifts of awareness from gross to subtle or causal states of consciousness.

Types: The major typology used in the Integral Warrior process is the masculine. We also examine the feminine because both must be integrated in each of us before we can truly awaken. We also use Jung's archetypes and typologies, among others, all valid types in Wilber's schema. Both masculine and feminine typologies are a major focus in awakening the new masculine, and we'll dive deeper into these types in a later chapter.

Picking up and reading Wilber can be challenging. A lot of the material is very dense and complicated, so I send different readers to different approaches to Wilber based on how I feel someone might fit into the AQAL model. One of the criteria I use is based on typologies. For instance, I feel there are distinct masculine and feminine paths to Wilber, so I might send someone who exhibits masculine tendencies to the book *A Theory of Everything.* I would send someone exhibiting more feminine traits to his book *Grace and Grit.*

Being an awakened man means being able to look at our world, others, and ourselves through the highest possible perspectives, including individually, collectively, subjectively, and intersubjectively. These serve as new lenses, if you will, about how our reality is put together. If you aren't looking at that world through the AQAL lens, you're missing the big picture. Wilber has provided me with more "aha" moments than any other path I've experienced, and while it might not do the same for you, its value as a tool for considering how we are growing in all aspects of our lives is unmatched. The question for all of us, then, becomes, What kind of future evolution do we want?

Small men have small perspectives. The Integral Warrior seeks to become a "big picture" man.

CHAPTER 4: MASTERING OPPORTUNITIES FOR CHANGE: DEVELOPMENTAL SYSTEMS THEORY AND SPIRAL DYNAMICS

I do suggest ... that for the overall welfare of total man's existence in the world, over the long run of time, higher levels are better than lower levels and that the prime good of any society's governing figures should be to promote human movement up the levels of human existence. —Clare Graves, *Spiral Dynamics,* p. 294

Putting their three dimensions (I, we, and it; or art, morals, and science; or Beauty, Goodness, and Truth) together with the major levels of existence would give us a much more genuinely integral or holistic approach to reality. —Ken Wilber

DEVELOPMENTAL PSYCHOLOGISTS, AND OTHERS, point out that it is usually "disorienting dilemmas" that are responsible for shifts in consciousness into later stages. It works because a situation arises that cannot be explained by the present level of consciousness, or development, of either the individual or the collective. Hence, an individual or a culture starts to expand viewpoints, usually looking closer at perspectives that would not have been considered at the earlier developmental stage.

Some psychologists and anthropologists point out that civilizations' major shifts occurred as a result of cultural and societal "disorienting dilemmas" that affected everyone, usually not in good ways, as the old dies to the new. But as the old ways die, newer ways, some better, emerge.

For several years, mostly on my blog, I've been pointing out that there are visible signs of major societal collapse all around us: peak oil, out-of-control population, climate change, pollution, drought, resource wars, terrorism (both by governments and others), the pathological rise of corporatism, and really ugly economics that simply cannot be hidden from view any longer. It is time to pay the piper.

All of this is also an opportunity to shift, to step up to the next level of human consciousness, learning from our mistakes—providing we have the time.

There are a lot of good developmental models out there. The simplest one I've seen is described in integral theory and has four stages of an evolutionary perspective: egocentric, ethnocentric, worldcentric, and cosmocentric. In each of these perspectives, growth is shown in ever-increasing circles of complexity, moving outward, each transcending and including the previous developmental stage. When one awakens to the world and cosmocentric stages, what is sometimes called the integral perspective, there is recognition that most of the global problems we face are a result of ego- and ethnocentric worldviews. While the problems of the planet must be addressed at the ego and ethnocentric levels, only solutions from the world and cosmocentric levels can solve them.

This simple developmental model holds true for individuals, organizations, cultures, and nations.

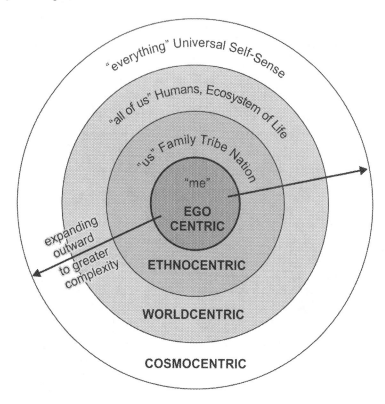

Figure 6

Figure 6 shows the natural movement from less complex worldviews transcending outward to more complex worldviews while including the previous levels. At each stage there is the capacity to destroy or evolve. The closer we get to cosmocentric, the more likely we are to solve the problems of the world. As the perspectives of each stage get larger, and the more our perspectives grow, our ability to see more clearly and take in more information and other perspectives increases. This allows us to shift perspectives and skills seamlessly to solve more complex problems.

Developmental Models

Developmental models, as we'll be describing them, are conceptual frameworks that draw on the key insights of what we know about theories of consciousness. Almost all of the key models agree that while people may progress through the stages of whatever model we're using at varying times, they generally pass through them in order, earlier to later. Some of the major models that are used in integral theory are Piaget's model of cognitive development,[44] Jane Loevinger and Susan Cook Greuter's Self-Sense and Leadership Maturity Framework,[45] Lawrence Kohlberg's stages of moral development,[46] Abraham Maslow's hierarchy of human needs,[47] and Clare Graves's "Emergent Cyclical Levels of Existence Theory,"[48] which later became known as Spiral Dynamics.[49]

All of the major developmental models—cognitive, self-sense, morals, needs, and values—examine a particular developmental line, as shown in Figure 7. Further, each of these lines unfolds in stages, or levels, but what are they levels of? What do they measure? The most obvious answer is levels of consciousness.

In other words, the levels of consciousness are actually the levels of development in each of the lines of development—and what is being developed in each of the lines is the amount of consciousness. As consciousness (or awareness) increases in a developmental line, it progresses to a higher level/wave/stage in the overall spectrum.

---

44   http://en.wikipedia.org/wiki/Piaget%27s_theory_of_cognitive_development
45   http://www.cook-greuter.com/
46   http://faculty.plts.edu/gpence/html/kohlberg.htm
47   http://www.abraham-maslow.com/m_motivation/Hierarchy_of_Needs.asp
48   http://www.clarewgraves.com/source_content/biography.htm
49   http://www.spiraldynamics.net/

Figure 7: Examples of Developmental Levels

	cognitive (Piaget, Aurobindo)	self-sense (Loevinger, Cook-Greuter)	morals (Kohlberg)	needs (Maslow)	values (Graves, Spiral Dynamics)
10	supermind	spirit-self	nondual (at manifestation)	Self-transcendence	platinum
9	overmind	soul-self	bodhisattvic (all sentient beings)		silver
8	intuitive mind	deeper psychic	post- post conventional		lavender
7	illumined mind	integrated (centaur)			coral
6	higher mind (vision-logic) — late / early	autonomous individualistic	Post-conventional	self-actualization	turquoise - cosmic awareness / yellow - systemic accepting
5	formal operational — late / early	conscientious	(my nation)	self-esteem	green - relativistic sociocratic / orange - achievement
4	concrete operational	conformist	conventional		Blue - absolutistic mythic
3		self-protective	my tribe	safety	red - egocentric power
2	preoperational	impulsive	pre-conventional (my self)		Purple - Magical animistic
1	sensorimotor	autistic		physiological	Beige - Survival

Spiral Dynamics

While all of the developmental lines are necessary, they are not, in and of themselves, sufficient. The integral model makes sure that we're paying attention to all of these lines and more. However, the primary developmental model used in the Integral Warrior workshop is Spiral Dynamics, based on the original work of Clare Graves. Graves was a professor of psychology at Union College in Schenectady, New York. There he developed an epistemological model of human psychology. Graves claimed that the inspiration for so doing came from undergraduate students in his introductory psychology course. He acknowledged that he was unable to answer the frequently asked question about who, from among the many competing psychology theorists, was ultimately "right" or "correct" with their model since there were elements of truth and error in all of them.[50]

Graves's work observed that the emergence within humans of new bio-psycho-social systems in response to the interplay of external conditions with neurology follows a hierarchy in several dimensions, though without guarantees as to timelines or even direction; both progression and regression are possibilities in his model. Consider the regression of the United States not long after the attacks of 9-11 and the impact of that regression on US foreign policy. Furthermore, each level in the hierarchy alternates as the human is either trying to make the environment adapt to the self or adapting the self to the existential conditions. He called these "express self" and "deny self" systems, and the swing between them is the cyclical aspect of his theory. Graves saw this process of stable plateaus interspersed with change intervals as never ending, up to the limits of the brain of *Homo sapiens,* something he viewed as far greater than we have yet imagined.

A number of management theorists and others have been influenced by Graves's "Emergent Cyclical Levels of Existence Theory." Chris Cowan and Don Beck used it as the basis for their book *Spiral Dynamics: Mastering Values, Leadership, and Change,*[51] which in turn is referenced by integral theorist Ken Wilber.

---

50   For more on Clare Graves, visit http://www.clarewgraves.com/home. html
51   Don Edward Beck and Christopher Cowan, *Spiral Dynamics: Mastering Values, Leadership, and Change* (Oxford, UK: Blackwell Publishing, 1996).

Don Beck has elaborated upon the work of his mentor, Clare Graves, to develop a multidimensional model for understanding the transformation of human *values and cultures*. As cofounder of the National Values Center in Denton, Texas, and CEO of the Spiral Dynamics Group, Inc., Beck travels widely, teaching the theory and practical applications of Spiral Dynamics Integral.[52]

Under Beck, the third iteration of the complex SDi material goes far beyond both earlier phases in striking out into new territory, in creating new strategic and systemic alliances, and in engaging academic and applied domains that are just now becoming part of the twenty-first century thought structures and existence problems. One of the distinguishing characteristics of SDi is the use of Wilber's AQAL model, which offers a user-friendly methodology for integrating Spiral Dynamics into personal, organizational, and societal operations.[53] "The model describes and makes sense of the enormous complexity of human existence," Dr. Don Beck says, "and then shows how to craft elegant, systemic problem–solutions that meet people and address situations where they are."

---

52 http://www.spiraldynamics.net/
53 http://www.spiraldynamics.net/about-spiral-dynamics-integral.html

Stage / Level	Color Code	Popular Name	Thinking	Cultural manifestations personal displays	
9	Coral			Too soon to say, but should tend to be I-oriented, controlling, consolidating if the pattern holds	Second Tier
8	Turquoise	WholeView	Holistic	Collective Individualaism, cosmic spirituality, earth changes	Second Tier
7	Yellow	FlexFlow	Ecological	Natural systems, self-principle, multiple realities, knowledge	Second Tier
6	Green	HumanBond	Consensus	Egalitarian, feelings, authentic, sharing, caring, community,	First Tier
5	Orange	StriveDrive	Strategic	Materialistic, success, consumerism, growth, image, status	First Tier
4	Blue	TruthForce	Authority	Meaning, discipline, tradition, morality rules; lives for later	First Tier
3	Red	PowerGods	Egocentric	Gratification, glitz, conquest, action, impulsive; lives for now	First Tier
2	Purple	KinSpirits	Animistic	Rite, rituals, taboos, superstition, tribes, folkways & Lore	First Tier
1	Beige	SurvivalSense	Instinctive	Food, water, procreation, warmth, protection, stays alive	First Tier

Figure 8

Why is it that people, family members, colleagues, companies, and governments appear to think in very different ways? Spiral Dynamics describes how new levels of consciousness emerge and flow through individuals and groups. It shows the following:

- How people think about things

- Why people make decisions in different ways

- Why people respond to different motivators

- Why and how values arise and spread

- The nature of change

It describes bio-psycho-social systems that form an expanding spiral along a continuum. Spiral Dynamics presents eight stages, or levels, of consciousness that have emerged on the planet, beginning with the survival level of consciousness and finishing off—so far—at the eighth level, holistic. These stages, which can also be thought of as the basic landmarks of the spiral, are represented by colors in the spiral diagram—beige, purple, red, blue, orange, green, yellow, turquoise, and the speculative ninth level, coral, with others to come (see Figure 8).

Between these landmark value or cultural levels are subsystems in which the ways of thinking, or worldview, are transitioning to the next level of consciousness, represented by the colors blending together:

- Some, like business people, are in the orange-to-green transition, seeking a return to more community and spirit in their lives.

- A number of politicians are in the blue-to-orange range, trying to move from structured bureaucracy to entrepreneurism and free markets.

- Many activists are living in the green-to-yellow zone as they work to achieve positive results on a human scale through interaction, involvement, and purposeful learning and teaching.

- Some developing regions are still in the purple-to-red transition as ancient tribal ways confront well-armed dictators, while others are in the red-to-blue area as a centralized authority tries to contain fractional battles.[54]

Spiral Dynamics and Change

As we can see from Figure 8, each level, or *meme*, on the spiral has traits that are unique to it. From a Spiral Dynamics perspective, change is inevitable because life conditions and human capacities are not fixed and are always changing. Alterations in either life conditions or human capacities can awaken new memes because of increasing complexities

54   A Mini-Course in Spiral Dynamics, http://www.spiraldynamics.org/learning/intro2SD.pdf

and the need to meet the challenges of an increasingly complex milieu. However, as Graves pointed out, "Change is not the rule; lack of change is not the rule." There are no guarantees.

When we experience "change" by repairing old systems, strengthening others, or even awakening new ones, the spiral will be distressed. Leaps forward are often preceded by desperate regression as older systems struggle to hold on. Here are some ways that memes find cognitive dissonance at each of the memetic levels:

- **Beige** experiences distress and delight based on biological satisfaction.

- **Purple** lives with fear and superstition.

- **Red** is caught up with anger and avoiding shame.

- **Blue** deals with an almost perpetual guilt burden.

- **Orange** is manic in its competitive urges to win in this life.

- **Green** caries great responsibility for others and the burden of caring so much.

- **Yellow**'s unemotional individualism is based on feelings about one's own performance and failures of systems to function as needed.

- **Turquoise** seems to reactivate outer-focused spirituality and Zen-like emotions based in liberation of consciousness without ceremony or "groupiness."[55]

The same things hold true for individuals and organizations. However comfortable we might be at whatever level we're at on the spiral, cognitive dissonance can create unanswered questions—questions that can no longer be answered by the values of our present level of thinking. Some examples of this are that the "truth" no longer guarantees order and the future as doubt, skepticism, and new options appear for Blue. For Orange,

---

55   Don Edward Beck and Christopher Cowan, *Spiral Dynamics: Mastering Values, Leadership, and Change,* 1996, p. 75.

the "good life" may be frayed and tarnished by consumptiveness as the rewards no longer provide inner peace or satisfaction. For Green, "Why can't we all get along?" wears thin and inadequate as complex societal problems and limited resources are laid bare; and last, Yellow's reliance on individual choices and freedom fails to provide the cooperative action necessary for overall survival.

The Integral Warrior workshop teaches a basic course in Spiral Dynamics because of its usefulness not only as an explanation for change but also as a *tool* for change, for awakening the new masculine. Spiral Dynamics is important in this context of the Integral Warrior because it teaches not only why people change but how they change. Understanding how and why we change helps men make the changes they need to make in their own lives in developing bigger, more complete perspectives of themselves and their world. Over thirty years ago, Graves wrote the following in "Human Nature Prepares for a Momentous Leap": [56]

> The present moment finds our society attempting to negotiate the most difficult, but at the same time the most exciting, transition the human race has faced to date. It is not merely a transition to a new level of existence but the start of a new "movement" in the symphony of human history. The future offers us, basically, three possibilities:
>
> 1) Most gruesome is the chance that we might fail to stabilize our world and, through successive catastrophes, regress as far back as the Ik tribe[57] has.
>
> 2) Only slightly less frightening is the vision of fixation in the [Blue/Orange/Green] societal complex. This might resemble George Orwell's *1984* with its tyrannical, manipulative government glossed over by a veneer of humanitarian sounding doublethink and moralistic rationalizations, and is a very real possibility in the next decades.

---

56   *The Futurist*, April, 1974.

57   Colin M. Turnbull, *The Mountain People* (New York: Touchstone Edition, 1987).

3) The last possibility is that a tipping point of 10% of the population could emerge into the next level of consciousness—yellow—and proceed toward stabilizing our world so that all life can continue.

The problems that confront us today stretch and challenge us to be bigger than we have been. Again, the levels of consciousness that created these problems cannot solve them. It will take a new man, a new woman, a new human, a new way of thinking, a new way of being. If we don't shift—if men don't step up and say, "Enough"—we may very well regress back to Beige, the survival level of consciousness, if we survive at all.

There's not enough space in the context of this book to get deeply into the complexities of Spiral Dynamics and its importance. I encourage you to learn more about this powerful tool.

The Integral Warrior understands the dynamics of change and that each level, when transcended, includes all the previous levels. In other words, as we develop, we bring all of the capacities forward with us. The Integral Warrior is able to call forth and use the characteristics of each of those levels from his higher perspective, as needed, for the good of all.

Chapter 5: Do We Really Need More Warrior Energy? The Path of the Integral Warrior

If someone granted you one wish, what do you imagine you would want out of life that you haven't gotten yet? For many people, it would be self-improvement and knowledge. That may well be why you're reading this now. What I've found is that, for me, the best way to learn something better is to teach it to someone else. It forces me to learn, assuming I am motivated enough to share my knowledge.

Because I am passionate about wanting to know more about the masculine and how we can best change, evolve, and grow spiritually, I decided to begin teaching it in the framework I created, the Integral Warrior. And while I still continue to learn every day and know that I have a much longer road to travel, it's working. I now have men attending my workshops on a regular basis who tell me how powerful this process is, and I'm able to see the shift that men make. Not only that, but their partners almost immediately notice the changes as well.

I understand that there are other ways this can happen, but this framework is the one I've created out of my own evolution through the many different processes and experiences I've had throughout the years and continue to have to this day. Therefore, I present it in the context of the Integral Warrior workshops I continue to facilitate around the country. In the next chapter, I'll elaborate on why I believe that the company of other men is so critical to this masculine healing process.

This new framework did not arise out of nothingness. It wasn't channeled, and it didn't come to me in a vision. It appears here because so many who have come before me have contributed so much. I have synthesized this new framework out of a whole slew of other framework parts that came before me and added in my own revelations, discoveries, intuition, and style. I have been blessed with the ability to work hard and to put it all together in a new form.

Much of my writing[58] has been about integral philosophy, the work of philosopher Ken Wilber,[59] and how it has affected my life. Now I'm moving into bringing this work into the world in a more powerful way—work that I believe is necessary. This work, of course, will always be informed by the integral model and Spiral Dynamics Integral but is no longer the focus of my workshops and writing; rather, it is an integral part of a larger picture. This larger vision, which is a combination of cognitive and experiential processes that assist in not only helping men understand the how and why of change but also to actually experience what it feels like to move into ever-increasing, expanding circles of evolutionary consciousness and complexity.

The main focus of the Integral Warrior workshop is on preparing men for and assisting them with the huge leap from the second to the third stage, or, in Spiral Dynamics jargon, the momentous leap from first tier to second tier. The vast majority of men in the Western world reside at Deida's first-stage masculine, with about 20 to 25 percent at second stage and perhaps 1 to 2 percent of men beginning to emerge into third-stage masculine.[60] You've already read about Deida's model in the first chapter, "What Is the New Masculine?" Historically, we know that any shift in consciousness from one stage to another requires about 10 percent of the population to reach the new stage. The 1960s were a

---

58   The Spiraling Universe, http:// www.garystamper.blogspot.com
59   http://www.beliefnet.com/Holistic-Living/2004/03/Who-Is-Ken-Wilber.aspx
60   Global Values Network: uses Spiral Dynamics to look at vMEMETIC cultural shifts on a global level.

perfect example of a new consciousness reaching a tipping point of 10 percent of the population and the impact of that shift.

Is your life seemingly more complicated and challenging than it used to be? Are you feeling a sense of urgency that you can't explain or calm? Does it seem that things aren't as you think they should be? Does it seem harder to enjoy life than it used to be? Are you feeling anxious, too busy, obsessive, and tense? Does it seem that more and more people you know are experiencing the same feelings?

Well, believe it or not, these feelings are a sign that something positive is about to happen to you. They are by-products of a consciousness shift, an awakening into new levels of understanding and awareness. They are also a challenge for us to let go of old ways of thinking that no longer serve us. This is not a sudden shift but a process, in shamanic terms, of dying to the old and being reborn to the new. During this process, everything is amplified, including our emotions.

Men who pay attention to these symptoms intuitively realize that something needs to shift. The question is, "How?" What can be done to speed up this evolutionary process, and how do we deal with the emotional roller coaster ride that comes with all this cognitive dissonance? How do we prepare to transform into this third-stage masculinity that empowers us in a way that serves the planet and our own freedom? Reintegration of the healthy masculine while maintaining our opposite aspect, the feminine, is a critical element in this process and in our spiritual evolution, individually and collectively. The degree to which we reject or are unable to access either is the degree to which we will stunt our growth in our "native" aspect.[61]

For the first time in the history of civilization, we now have access to all of the wisdom traditions, philosophies, and religions that have preceded us, including the ones that exist in the postmodern world. The question is no longer whether we have the ability and tools we need to improve our lives, the lives of our loved ones, and the planet. The question now is, "Do we have the will?"

---

61 Jim Benson, The Awakened Masculine, http:// www. awakenedmasculine.com

I deeply understand this at this time in my life because I'm going through it right now, even as I complete this book. I can see where I need to go but cannot fully embody it. I can see what I need to let go of and can't surrender to it. That is my task at my current place on the evolutionary spiral. It's not something you do once and you're done—it's something that hopefully happens no matter where you are on the wheel. It's how we continue to grow—in a continuous series of challenges and then by rising up and meeting those challenges.

The Learning Tool of the Integral Warrior

The Integral Warrior men's workshop is a six-weekend process that takes place over several months' time. The process combines Jungian and emerging archetypes; cutting-edge integral and developmental systems theory; ancient shamanic wisdom traditions of altered-state consciousness technologies like the Shamanic Breathwork Process and journeying, meditation, guided imagery, and shamanic death and rebirth; and ritual and deeply thought-out initiations.

One of the emergent qualities of this combination of practices and teachings is how the altered-state (experiential) and cognitive work anchor each other, the being and the doing, and burn the experiences into the awareness of the participants. Another is how the other developmental model I use, Spiral Dynamics Integral,[62] relates to the development of each of the four primary Jungian archetypes.[63]

This combination of tools, modern and ancient, available to humanity for the first time in its fullness, creates a new paradigm of learning and healing that provides new awareness of who we are, why we do what we do, and where we're headed and helps men move toward new structures of consciousness. By building a stronger existing foundation (translational, or horizontal development), we create bridges to the next stage (transformational, or vertical development) that allow whatever shift is needed to begin emerging in just a few months, a process that generally takes years to unfold, if it is to happen at all.

---

62   Don Edward Beck and Christopher C. Cowan, *Spiral Dynamics*, 1996.
63   See Chapter 9.

While the primary goal of the Integral Warrior is to prepare men to move toward third-stage masculine, the process is developmentally neutral. That is, it works at whatever level of consciousness the participant is.[64] We have what we need to be the models for this emerging consciousness. As the sayings go, "If not now, when? If not you, who?" and "We are the ones we've been waiting for." What does the process look like? Here's a brief overview of the seven segments that move men into new ways of thinking and being:

Integral Warrior Modules

The Mankind Project provides men with a way to move from first-stage to second-stage masculine. That is incredibly important and necessary work. MKP provides a solid base that the Integral Warrior builds on. I've had many MKP men in my Integral Warrior workshops who value both and who say that the Integral Warrior takes them deeper into their quest for the new masculine. It's designed to do that. The Integral Warrior process's purpose is to begin to move men from second-stage to third-stage masculine. It generally does this in seven two-day weekends, spread out over approximately one weekend a month, or three four-day segments consisting of two modules each, and the modules are intense but enjoyable. They are meant to bring our stuff up and expose it to the light.

Module One is a special introductory weekend designed to allow men to experience the shadow of the King archetype within and the Shamanic Priest Process before committing to the entire journey. It consists of introductions to the major Jungian archetypes: King, Warrior, Magician, Lover. It addresses what the Divine Masculine is and why it is so important, and it provides an introduction to integral theory and the Spiral Dynamics developmental model. Participants learn about how the masculine grows and why and are led on a shamanic journey into their psyches. The weekend also includes a beginning exploration into the King archetype, the definition of *initiation* and an explanation

---

64   This assumes that the participants are at the rational/scientific/achiever level of development or higher. If a man is not, I recommend that he look into the Mankind Project.

on why it is so critical, and an overview of the remaining process and weekends.

At the end of the introductory weekend, men have an opportunity to decide whether or not they want to experience the full process, consisting of an additional six weekends.

Module Two includes the following:

- The first of *the four initiations*, the Warrior archetype, and initiation and emergence of the Spiritual Warrior—having this archetype on board from the beginning gives men the drive to complete the rest of the process

- Finding your purpose, integrity, and authenticity and standing firm for what you believe is right

- A deeper look into integral theory, lines, states and stages, and Spiral Dynamics

- Guided imagery on Warrior past lives and the shadow of the warrior

- Discovering your deepest purpose and your mission

- Nine steps to becoming the Spiritual Warrior

- Claiming the Spiritual Warrior archetype through ritual and initiation

During Module Three, participants delve into these areas:

- The Lover archetype, finding your inner beloved, and balancing masculine and feminine energies

- Learning how to embody the Lover

- Developing empathy and compassion through Open Heart practices

- The light and shadow of the Lover, how they are both gifts

- A deeper exploration of integral theory

- Big-Mind meditation, including shifting awareness of your inner landscape and experiential awareness of nondual realization

- Claiming the Lover archetype through ritual and the second initiation

Module Four leads men to an understanding of the following:

- The Magician archetype and why the Shamanic Priest is the fullest expression of the Magician

- Balancing the seen and unseen dimensions

- Ministering to the world

- Accepting the mantle of spiritual leadership

- Creating and holding sacred space

- The Magician's relationship to the King and the Lover

- Discovering what you need and what's needed on the planet at this time

- Claiming the Magician archetype through ritual and the third initiation

In Module Five, we explore:

- Shamanic astrology archetypes, accessing our Mars to get closer to our masculine and our Moon and Venus to learn how to access the Goddess (feminine) within

- Accessing the mediating energies between heaven and earth to allow us to feel our divinity connected to our humanity

- The elements and the cycles of change, instruction that provides the necessary background should a man wish to be an ordained minister in the shamanic lineage

- How to better comprehend and embrace the essence of our original intent, while consciously dreaming the dream forward

- The personal and political rant

- Sacred Marriage of the masculine and feminine

By Module Six, participants are exposed to these subjects:

- The 3-2-1 Shadow Process, used to identify personal shadows

- The Shamanic Breathwork Process, sacred art, and initiation to travel between the seen and unseen to clear the blockages that prevent your King from emerging in his fullest manifestation, balancing and integrating the other archetypes so that each is fully accessible as needed

- Death of the old King ritual

- The fourth initiation: The birth of the new King

Finally, in Module Seven, the final weekend, participants prepare for a self-proclaiming ceremony for the emergence of the Shamanic Priest and Integral Warrior, which is witnessed by friends and family.

In addition, each of the weekends is rich with the personal stories of the men who participate, shadow and light, and life experiences and histories of their relationships with the archetypes of the King, Warrior, Lover, and Magician and their own lives.

If you can't attend an Integral Warrior workshop in your area, or travel to where one is, the next best thing would be to form your own group of like-minded men and share this book and the practices contained within. A men's group, with scheduled, committed meetings, is important for several reasons that we'll delve into in the next chapter.

Why the Warrior?

Some people have asked why I call my men's workshop the Integral

Warrior, saying, "We've had too much warrior energy on the planet and look where it's gotten us." The warrior energy those people are referring to is that of the old warrior—the unquestioning soldier. The new warrior, the one who stays awake and alert, who questions authority, the awakened masculine, is exactly what we need today if we are to survive as a species and shift to the awakening that has been prophesied for ages—sometimes called "the great shift," "the planetary ascension," "the quickening," "an evolutionary leap," and more recently, "awakening to the new consciousness." Today's new warrior fights the battle within, fighting himself. The Integral Warrior's principles are inner peace, tranquility, love, power, strength, honor, majesty, and respect—and we have to fight for these principles, for no freedom is free.

The problems we face today require the decisive action of the Warrior, who moves fearlessly into the void, tempered by the Lover's heart, the Magician's skill, and the King's big-picture consciousness. If, as some people think, we repress the Warrior, it goes into shadow and will eventually reemerge in unhealthy and even sociopathic ways.

In the following chapters, we'll touch on the tools of the shaman and the role those tools play in what's being called post-postmodernism—for lack of a better term—or reaching second-tier consciousness, third-stage masculine. We'll also introduce a couple of different ways to create sacred space and include some altered state practices, including guided imagery and the Shamanic Breathwork Process, the best shadow tool I've ever come across.

In addition, we'll also dive into the four primary masculine archetypes, the importance of ritual and initiation in men's lives, and the work that brings them all forward together, creating the Path of the Integral Warrior.

Chapter 6: Setting Up the Container: Creating Sacred Space

Whenever we moderns pause for a moment, and enter the silence, and listen very carefully, the glimmer of our deepest nature begins to shine forth, and we are introduced to the mysteries of the deep, the call of the within, the infinite radiance of a splendor that time and space forgot. We are introduced to the all-pervading Spiritual domain that the growing tip of our honored ancestors were the first to discover. And they were good enough to leave us a general map to that infinite domain, a map called the Great Nest of Being, a map of our own interiors, an archeology of our own Spirit. —Ken Wilber[65]

THE FIRST WEEKEND OF the Integral Warrior is an introductory weekend designed to allow men to get a taste of the process before committing to the entire journey. It consists of introductions to the major Jungian archetypes—King, Warrior, Magician, Lover—and an introduction to integral theory (the most comprehensive map of human consciousness yet) and the Spiral Dynamics developmental model. This powerful introduction is largely about how the masculine grows, and why, because this understanding is essential in aiding our own growth. The weekend also includes a guided shamanic journey into our psyches, a beginning exploration into the shadow of the King archetype and

---

65   Ken Wilber, Integral Psychology: Consciousness, Spirit, Psychology, Therapy (Boston: Shambhala Publications, 2000), p. 190.

the death of the old King, a look at what initiation is and why it is so critical, and an overview of the remaining process and weekends. Men can attend that weekend as a stand-alone weekend if they want; at the end of the weekend, they have the opportunity to decide whether or not they want to commit to experiencing the full process, consisting of an additional six weekends.

During the writing of this book, I realized I would not be able to put the entire process into a single book. That became obvious to me when I had completed four chapters on the process and hadn't even finished the first day of the first of six weekends. So the first section of this work is set up much like the introductory weekend. I'll give you the first weekend in detail and then an overview of the rest of the process with some practices over the remainder of the book.

The Integral Warrior process unfolds best in the presence and with the support of other men. Again, if you can't attend an Integral Warrior workshop in your area, then you should get together with a group of like-minded men, sharing the book and the practices contained within. I cannot overemphasize the importance of doing this process with other men. The support, accountability, dedication, and ultimately the healing that can be provided by other men is one of the keys of the transformation that takes place through the process.

Here are some of the reasons a men's group is so important:[66]

1. **Rubber Banding:** Men and women know how hard it is to follow through with deep, spiritual teachings in their everyday lives without any kind of support. I can't tell you how many times I've experienced the so-called rubber band effect after attending a great and profound workshop. "Rubber-banding" occurs when you get stretched open, beyond your normal boundaries, in a challenging or ecstatic situation but then "snap back" to your more habitual patterns of behavior when you return to your everyday life. This is also known as a "state," or temporary, experience. Without

---

66 Taken from David Deida, *The Way of the Superior Man: A Spiritual Guide to Mastering the Challenges of Women, Work, and Sexual Desire* (Boulder, CO: Sounds True, 1997).

being able to embody the temporary experience, we go right back to being who we were before the weekend. A men's group provides a conscious community to support men's continued growth of deep understanding and practice. A caveat to this is that the more state experiences we have, the easier it is to move to the next stage, or a permanent structure of consciousness.

2. **Being in the Company of Other Men:** Men discover and refine their purpose by being in solitude in the challenges they meet, but something happens in the presence of other men that seemingly can't happen alone or in the company of the feminine, especially when those men won't settle for bullshit. A man's capacity to receive another man's direct criticism is a measure of his capacity to receive masculine energy.

3. **Having Men Hold You Accountable for Living Your Deepest Purpose:** Unless you know your mission and have aligned your life to it, your core will feel empty. Your presence in the world will be diminished, as will your presence with your intimate partner and with other men. Other men will challenge you to stay focused on your mission, and your purpose should take priority over everything else in your life.

4. **Men Who Are Dedicated with You:** Choose to be in the company of other men who have dedicated their lives to integrity, truth, and the heart—men who are dedicated to live with an open heart and give their deepest gifts of love, mission, and presence. The way a conscious man penetrates the world should be the same way he penetrates his woman—not merely for personal gain or pleasure but to magnify love, openness, and depth

5. **Support Your Edge with Other Men:** Choose male friends who are themselves living at their edge, facing their fears and living just beyond them. Men of this kind can love you

without protecting you from the necessary confrontation with reality.

6. **Cut through Your BS:** At least once a week, get together with your male friends to serve one another. Cut through the bullshit and talk straight with each other. Welcome such criticisms from your friends. Suggest challenges for each other to take on in order to bring each other through the fears that limit your surrender in gifting.

Awakening the new masculine, like the Integral Warrior workshop, consists of a set of processes, both experiential and cognitive. The introductory weekend of the Integral Warrior process sets the tone for all of the remaining weekends and creates the safety and sacred space that must be present for transformation to take place, both in the first and subsequent weekends. This safety, in the context of sacred space, provides men with the ability to tell the truth—about themselves, their shortcomings, their wounds, their strengths, and their shadows, dark and light—and one another.

Creating safety in men's groups is critical. We've been taught not to trust other men, to shut down our emotions, to close down and to "man up." There are proven ways to help men create a safe and sacred space in which they can begin to open up with other men. But there's more—necessary in building trust and creating openness and safety where transformation can take place are a set of conditions that must be addressed and agreed upon by the men. These agreements, known as the Three C's, are as follows:

1. **Commitment**: Men engaged in opening up and talking about, often for the first time, their deepest fears, their true aspirations, who they really are, how powerful they might truly be, and what's going on with them can become fearful as the old ways struggle to hold as they begin to drop away. Sometimes there can be a tendency to want to run when the earlier structure's thinking and feeling begin to crumble. The commitment is to not leave the group or sessions without talking to the facilitator or leader of the group. While the fear and the desire to run from what can

arise when doing deep work can be very real, the actual departure rarely happens. Still, the agreement is important. As the process continues after the first weekend, men begin to rely on each other for support, and to leave the group after two or three weekends would create a hole in the group and reinforce the old brain feeling that other men cannot be trusted.

2. **Chemicals:** The Integral Warrior process also uses altered-state methods like the Shamanic Breathwork Process,[67] so it's important to stay away from consciousness-altering substances—drugs and alcohol, specifically—for a day or two before and after journeying. When we step into these altered-state experiences, we don't want another altered state competing with the work we've done. I've often had men ask me if caffeine and tobacco are okay or if they should also be avoided. I've found that when men are asked to stop either, even for a couple of days, they can enter a far more disruptive withdrawal state than if they continue with them, seriously affecting their ability to journey, so I don't suggest stopping their usage. I've also found that stopping my use of caffeine can be disruptive!

3. **Confidentiality**: Critical to creating a safe container is the old adage, "What happens in Vegas stays in Vegas." Anyone who is going to deeply open up to reveal their inner-most workings, shadows, fears, family of origin wounds, etc., needs to know they won't be ridiculed, or have someone talking about them outside of the group. My general approach is that it's okay to talk about your own processes outside of the group but not anyone else's.

After I've explained to the group what each of the Three C's are. I then ask them, "Do you agree with these conditions?" I then wait until I've had a "yes" from each man. I've never received a "no," but if I did, I would stop and ask why to see if I could support his reasons. If, in the end, a man could not agree to all of the conditions, I would have to

---

67   See Chapter 8.

thank him for his honesty and ask him to leave the group. There could be several reasons that a man might not agree to the Three C's. Some men are commitment-phobic and simply cannot commit because of their fear of the unknown, usually as a result of their inner landscape or childhood wounds. Some men have addiction-related dependencies that haven't been addressed, and a twelve-step program might be a better use of their, and my, time. Last, some men simply don't have the developmental maturity to do this work, and they are, quite frankly, not called to the Integral Warrior.[68]

Creating Sacred Space

The work of the Integral Warrior, and the approach it takes in awakening the new masculine, is a decidedly spiritual practice. To do the work, we recognize that there is something larger than ourselves at play here. At this level of spiritual awareness, the men I work with have either acknowledged or are in the process of acknowledging that the old, archaic, magical, and mythical representations of God no longer hold any answers to the questions of Spirit. Many of them are also moving beyond a rational or a pluralistic God, perhaps not yet articulating but unconsciously understanding that our concepts of God, or Spirit, evolves as we evolve. This evolution is what Wilber calls a "conveyor belt" of spirituality that moves us from an egocentric to an ethnocentric to a worldcentric and ultimately to a cosmocentric worldview. While we do not have to be "religious" to experience any of these stages, it does, however, turn out that religion is the "only institution in all of humanity's endeavors that can actually do this."[69]

While the men who are called to this path are usually more spiritual than religious, it's important to acknowledge that religion, in any form, is simply institutionalized spirituality.

The Integral Warrior process uses an awareness of Spirit, by whatever name we want to call it, to help hasten our evolution by tapping into our deepest "I," our highest and most meaningful selves. It does this

---

68   The Integral Warrior is intended to move men from second-stage to third-stage masculine.
69   Ken Wilber, *Integral Spirituality*, 2006, p. 210.

through meditations, guided journeys, and experiential practices that create altered states of consciousness that allow us to listen more deeply, speak more thoughtfully, and be more aware, or conscious.

This is also the shaman, the master of subtle state consciousness, taking participants in the process to deeper levels of being.

I start off each weekend with dance and stretching. The music comes from a variety of sources and has a definite masculine slant. We dance about ten minutes to songs like Sly and the Family Stone's "Stand," the Neville Brothers' "Fly Like an Eagle," and the Agape Choir's "Make Me an Instrument"—all up-tempo grooves that speak to the masculine slant and power. For a lot of men, this is the first time they've ever danced just with other men, and they can be tentative at first. But they soon warm up, often doing exercise moves, which are fine. The dance also loosens everyone up and begins to allow the participants to settle in.

The process of setting up and creating sacred space has already begun at this point. There are lots of ways to open sacred space, but my two favorite ways are calling in the directions and expanding awareness of the group's collective unconsciousness. The first creates the space of the ecosphere, the physical plane and its connection to Spirit. The second, diving into the collective field of luminous energy, creates the space of the noosphere to share the vision of the fulfillment of humanity's highest potential. It is this part of us that is always one with God.

Let's first touch on calling in the directions.

In the sacred space created by calling in the directions, our awareness moves beyond our small "s" selves and embraces all of creation. Some of the men have never called in the directions before, so I provide them with a script that we use until they are comfortable enough to call in the directions without it. Calling in the directions begins with "smudging" the room, fanning smoldering sage or incense in the four directions, and then smudging each of the men, releasing any and all outside influences, distractions, emotions that don't serve them or others, and whatever might be getting in our way of connecting with Spirit on the physical or spiritual plane. Smudging is also used to call in our allies, our ancestors, angels, anything that watches over us, holding the openings of our deepest and fullest expression of ourselves, and protects us.

Then, standing in the first direction, with arms and hands facing outward as if to touch the direction, each man recites the verse for the appropriate direction, calling upon the archetype of that direction. But these archetypes are more than just symbols; they are primordial energies or spirits with lives and powers of their own, and we ask for their knowledge and their power to guide and assist us in creating the sacred space.

With an intentional masculine approach, I created this calling in the directions that moves as the masculine moves, on purpose and singularly focused, as one part of my approach to integral shamanism. Because the Integral Warrior uses Jungian archetypes; I also brought in the King, Warrior, Magician, and Lover archetypes into the calling.

The East

We call in the Spirit-keepers of the East, place of the rising sun, the archetype of the Warrior and the element of fire—the place of the dawn, new beginnings, vision and inspiration of newness and fresh starts. The eye of the eagle, able to see the big picture, the place of creativity, cocreation, and conscious leadership. We call in the energies of the east, new beginnings, and questions needing answers. What are we at the beginning of? What have we just begun to figure out? What visions and plans are we creating? We call in burning through our fears and blockages to stand in our truth and our light as spiritual Warriors. Welcome Spirit-keepers of the East.

The South

We call in the Spirit-keepers of the South, the archetype of the King and the element of water. We call in the energy of plans getting established and projects coming to life, the realization of visions and plans of the East. We call in the energy of organizing and making things happen, diligence and small steps—the middle, the working time, the everyday ongoing flow of effort, of purpose, of our mission. We call in mouse energy, scurrying around, tending to small tasks. We call in the ability to stand and feel all the aspects of our lives that are in full swing, living in the South. Welcome Spirit-keepers of the South.

The West

We call in the Spirit-keepers of the West and the setting sun, the archetype of the Lover and conscious relationship, the element of air, the place of harvest and abundance, of sharing and community, accomplishment and enjoyment, time for sharing the bounty of our efforts and connecting with others. We call in personal introspection: What have we learned from whatever we just finished? What might we do differently next time? It's the place to celebrate and take stock of our lives. The West has otter energy, whimsical and relaxed, playing through the forest and the water. And like the otter, the West heads into the hibernation of the North. Welcome Spirit-keepers of the West.

The North

We call in the Spirit-keepers of the North, the nighttime sky, the archetype of the Priest—the Magician—and the element of earth, the place of sleeping and dreaming, solitude and spiritual introspection, connecting with Spirit, of communing with unseen worlds, deep inner reflection, meditation, and receiving guidance. It is the place of the night, winter, and the wisdom of the elder, of celebration and taking stock of the Spirit that moves through all things. The North is bear energy, fully embracing the night and the visions that are gestating in hibernation, and in the dawn before the dawn, we begin to feel the stirrings of the next phase. Welcome Spirit-keepers of the North.

The Above, the Below, and the Center

We call in the center and the three final energies: Father Sky, Mother Earth, and our own essence. Father Sky is consistent, reliable, and predictable. We call in the masculine energies that are stable and strong, the place of order and discipline. We call in Mother Earth—beautiful, spontaneous, ever-changing, always in motion, never the same from one moment to the next, the good feminine energies of Mother Earth, adaptable, flexible, inspirational, and creative. Finally, we call in our own essence, feeling into our cores, feeling the part of the universe that is only and totally filled with us, connecting to the energies of our own uniqueness, our special medicine, our songs, our gifts. When we are filled with our own personal energetic energies, we walk on, taking within us the four directions, Father Sky, Mother Earth, and the fulfillment of all that we are. Welcome Spirit-keepers of the above, the below, and the center.

When the session or weekend and the healing work are done, it's important to close the sacred space following the same procedure, acknowledging the archetypes and the directions and thanking and releasing them. My wife taught me to say, "Stay if you will; go if you must."

Next, let's examine creating sacred space through the collective field of luminous energy.

There are many ways in which this can be done. Some will utilize the light of the eighth chakra, the *wiracocha*, which resides outside the physical body but within the luminous energy field. One of the best ways is a group practice called Insight Dialogue,[70] a process that was taught to me by one of my dearest teachers, Terri O'Fallon, one of the principals of the Seattle-based Pacific Integral and its leadership-based program, Generating Transformational Change in Human Systems.[71]

Insight Dialogue is a meditation practice bringing the qualities of deep meditation and interpersonal communication together. This sounds simple, but one soon discovers that an unpredictable depth and richness of experience is possible with Insight Dialogue. This combination of Insight Meditation and Bohmian Dialogue is, by far, the deepest, most powerful meditative experience I've ever had. Created by Terri and Gregory Kramer, Insight Dialogue is a process that can take us to another level of interpersonal communication. Within an altered-state

---

70   http://www.pacificintegral.com/workshops/idoverview.htm
71   http://pacificintegral.com/

meditative group process, we learn to address individual and group issues by audibly verbalizing what is coming through our individual and collective inner voices. The process creates an amazing field of shared consciousness between participants. "It is an engaged practice of deeply mindful interchange involving a natural resting in intrinsic awareness in which all phenomena arise and fall within oneself and within the community," O'Fallon says. "The inclination towards mindfulness while speaking and writing that is fostered in Insight Dialogue (ID) supports the practice of awareness during the complex tasks and social interchanges of day to day living and allows individuals practicing ID without other dialogic meditators to develop their own intrinsic awareness and to foster it in the people around them by example."

Insight Dialogue expands Insight Meditation and Bohmian Dialogue into interaction, turning conversation into a transformative, creative vehicle for something brand new and unanticipated to emerge into a deeper awareness. Here's how Insight Dialogue listening and speaking works in a nutshell:

- **Commit to the Process**—Bring your awareness to the present moment.

- **Pause**—Call forth to slow down, to drop ignorance, to see more deeply, and to brighten the mind.

- **Relax**—Call forth in the face of stress and of challenging truths to bring ease to the body-mind.

- **Open**—Call to move out of isolated practice, loops, and selfish patterns to be out of contraction.

- **Trust Emergence**—Call forth for energy, to end doubt, and to ride the moment.

- **Listen Deeply**—Call into inquiry and receptivity to extend the heart.

- **Speak the Truth**—Call forth to end stasis, to enhance generosity and courage, and to bring meditative interaction.

Consciously entering a shared, collective energy field, this amazing process allows men, sometimes for the very first time, to listen and speak directly from their hearts. While engaged in the process, the undeniable and palpable field of luminous energy makes it possible for men to open up without shame or fear of being judged by the other men.

Here's an induction for Insight Dialogue. It's designed to take a group deep into a comeditative, shared, altered-state space. You can either have a discussion agenda in mind or simply allow whatever wants to emerge come forth. With your group, come together in a circle, sitting in meditative posture. Dim the lights and have some soft, ethereal music playing in the background. Speaking in a soft voice, begin the Insight Dialogue induction or guided meditation.

Insight Dialogue Session

Insight Dialogue is a meditation practice that includes listening, speaking, and, in an online format, reading and writing. Since the best way to understand a practice is to experience it, I'd like to invite you to begin engaging in the practice right now by settling in, slowing down … and becoming aware of the changing sensations of the body as you sit listening to my voice or are reading these words. Notice any tensions … and invite them to relax.… Take the time to do this without striving … without judgment … Make sure you observe whether you've gotten caught up in your reactions to the words or in a passing thought or feeling … and take a moment to step back from that involvement.

Now bring your awareness to the activities of the mind … Notice any expectations that may be there regarding what you're about to hear … any biases … any thoughts or feelings still percolating from whatever activity preceded this one, any thoughts or feelings about what you'll be doing next … and begin to step back from these movements, relaxing into a deep and wide listening space.

As you continue to listen, observe any responses that may arise … any reaction of attraction or aversion, like or dislike … without becoming involved in them. When you find yourself becoming involved, then, without judgment, simply let go and step back once again into a wide and calm receptivity and attentiveness.

At any point, you might wish to check in with your experience ... becoming aware of thoughts ... feelings ... and sensations that have arisen ... and if you find yourself attached to or involved in any of them, take a moment to relax, step back, and regather the strands of your awareness into a one-pointed pause in the present moment.

Allow yourself to settle into the sensations of the physical body ... noticing any tensions that may be there and inviting them to relax ... noticing the panorama of thoughts, feelings, and sensations rising and falling, moment to moment ... allowing yourself to drift inward to a place of stillness and calm from which you can witness the passing show without being moved by it.

Begin to get a sense of the physical boundary of the body and a sense of the separate self that it seems to enclose. Allow that boundary to gradually soften and dissolve so all is now floating in a vast, unbounded field of conscious awareness ... very calm, very still, and infinitely compassionate.

Notice the movement of energy in this field of awareness ... movement that we experience as thoughts, feelings, and sensations ... arising out of stillness ... moving through stillness ... and merging again back into stillness.

Notice the tendency to grasp onto these movements as "my" thoughts, "my" feelings, and "my" sensations, and notice how the sense of a solid, separate self begins to congeal around that grasping, recreating "my" self-image.

Notice the shift between grasping and letting go ... between the tension and suffering that accompanies the grasping and the freedom and joy of letting go. And let it all be held with great tenderness, kindness, and compassion for the suffering of that apparent self that experiences itself as separate from the Divine and in all beings and all things.

As you read these words, I'd like to invite you to reflect on how they might be relevant to your experience in every moment.

Now, gently come back into the room, opening your eyes when you're ready, and bring your awareness to the activities of the mind ... Notice any expectations that may be there regarding what you're about to experience ... any biases ... any thoughts or feelings still percolating from the day, any thoughts or feelings about what you'll be doing next ... and just relax into a deep and wide listening space.

As we continue, observe any responses that may arise ... any reactions, attractions, aversions, likes or dislikes ... without becoming involved in them. When you find yourself becoming involved, simply let go and step back into that wide and calm listening and speaking space.

... And when you're ready, simply let the dialogue begin.

Missteps and Misconceptions around Insight Dialogue

There are two primary ways that an Insight Dialogue session can go astray. One lies in the tendency to become caught up in the sweetness of sharing and empathizing with another's emotional experience, perhaps offering kind and well-intentioned words of solace or advice. While an entirely worthy and often healing function of group engagement, this is not the purpose of insight dialogue. In Insight Dialogue, we observe our tendency to get caught up in another's identification with the movements of their vital nature—whether higher or lower—and attempt to step back from them. By retreating into an inner stillness, we can be with the person in loving kindness while seeing his experience as part of the ebb and flow of universal tides, thus inviting him to do the same. In this way, we continually support each other in choosing the path of freedom—turning away from the smallness and suffering of our reactive nature and toward the fullness and joy of our true being. And thus do we create an ideal setting in which purification and eventual psychic transformation of the outer nature can be nurtured.

The other tendency is to be drawn into an intellectual conversation, getting caught up in what may well be a fresh and compelling flow of ideas. Again, this is an immensely valuable and invigorating pursuit. However, if we do not engage these ideas with the calm mind, we may remain blind to a host of conditioned and largely subconscious habits, which, from the shadows, control what we think, feel, and say. It is bringing these habits to awareness in the interest of freeing ourselves from them that is the particular province of insight dialogue. From the depths of inner stillness emerges the possibility of a yet richer, more creative, and more intuitive discourse liberated from the knots of karmic compulsion.

Insight Dialogue is not just a conversation in which everyone speaks more slowly and pauses often. The space, pacing, and pausing are skillful means of creating the space we need to stay mindful of our experience, stay in the present moment, and continually take refuge in the calm of our inner being.

We also want to be careful not to get caught up in our stories, philosophies, or mental abstractions. The idea is to maintain inner stillness and a deep state of listening while being aware of what is being said. Last, Insight Dialogue is not a strictly regulated conversation with rigid rules. The guidelines are designed to help us be aware and conscious of the speaking and listening habits that normally escape us, freeing us of our reactivity and liberating us from our past conditioning so that we are free to meet and engage—"I with Thou, on the Sacred ground of Love and mutual self-knowing."[72]

I generally use this process as we step into telling our stories about who we are for the first time in the group. For most men, this is the first time they've ever spoken or listened this deeply, and the effects of having their hearts opened through this process are profound and sacred.

To learn more about Insight Dialogue, see Gregory Kramer's book, *Insight Dialogue: The Interpersonal Path to Freedom.*[73]

More about Sacred Space

In my Integral Warrior workshops, sacred space must be reestablished on each of the seven weekends and at the beginning of each day. I generally will use Insight Dialogue on more than one day as it allows men to get more comfortable and familiar with it. I also use a variety of guided meditations, including some I wrote myself and some that I

---

72   Used with permission from Terri O'Fallon, Pacific Integral.
73   http://www.amazon.com/dp/1590304853/?tag=gooyhdr-20&hvadid=3656372207&ref=pd_sl_83b2t2fuga_b

create in the moment that arise spontaneously because there's something that needs to emerge.

Following are some other meditations I use in the process:

- Genpo Roshi's Big Mind, Big Heart,[74] a guided process that is astonishingly original, profound, and an effective path for waking up, or seeing one's own true nature

- Ken Wilber's "I Amness" meditation, from *The Integral Vision*, p. 221

- Tonglen Tibetan Buddhist meditation: Compassion and loving-kindness teaches us that before we can have compassion for others, we must first have compassion for ourselves

- The Inner Shaman Meditation, adapted from Jungian psychology's "active imagination" exercise and using guided imagery in free-form visualization (more on this in Chapter 8).

You can, and should, make a sacred space in your own home or in your day as a practice. Sacred space can be as small as a breath taken during prayer or meditation, as large as a cathedral, or as expansive as an ocean view. Consider setting up an altar in your home in a corner, a spare bedroom, or even a closet. Once you've chosen the space, clear it of everything. Perhaps you'll repaint it. Select pleasing visuals, scents, objects, cloths, sounds, and kinesthetics[75] for your surroundings.

My sacred space is filled with objects that I've collected throughout the years that have special and sacred meaning for me: a mask from Chichen Itza, a small statuette of Buddha, seashells from a favorite beach, a rock from a fire pit that I fire walked on, a Native American flute, a statue, candles, incense, gifts from loving friends and family, a broken arrow from a ceremony, flowers, and much more. It's important to perform a ritual or ceremony of your choice to dedicate and honor your sacred

---

74   Dennis Genpo Merzel, *Big Mind, Big Heart: Finding Your Way* (Maclean, VA: Big Mind Publishing, 2007).

75   The ability to feel movements of the limbs and body.

space. You could light candles or some incense and bless your space in whatever way honors you and your belief systems.

Whether your sacred space contains all of the items I've mentioned or just a solitary object such as a statue or sculpture, your space is a place to be reborn and renewed every day. It's about drawing yourself inward and getting closer to what's in your heart.

It doesn't matter if the sacred space is in the privacy of your home or created with and for a group of people. Sacred space is a healing sphere that is pure, holy, and safe. Within sacred space, everyone is protected. This, too, is the way of the Integral Warrior.

Chapter 7: Integral Shamanism: Moving from Magic to the Transpersonal

We do not know where death awaits us: so let us wait for it everywhere. To practice death is to practice freedom. A man who has learned how to die has unlearned how to be a slave.
—Montaigne

Your ancestors were shamans: every one comes from a shamanic culture. —John Perkins

SHAMANISM IS AN ANTHROPOLOGICAL term referencing a wide range of beliefs and practices around communication with the spiritual world, which, in turn, affects the human world. Practitioners of shamanism, known as shamans, are found across multiple cultures and continents and millennia. Shamans existed in many forms and cultures, some of which may have originated as early as the Paleolithic period, with its peak period probably from around 50,000 to 7,000 BCE. Shamanism existed long before the first religions emerged.

In most cultures, shamanism holds that shamans are intermediaries between the spirit world and the world of humans. It is said that shamans walk between the worlds and can treat illnesses and ailments by mending the soul. Healing these illnesses and traumas, which affect the soul or spirit, restores the physical body to balance and wholeness.

Shamans also enter the spirit world to solve community problems, bring guidance to misguided souls, or to identify and resolve issues caused by foreign elements.

Shamanism has traditionally been a "calling" and is generally involuntary. Individuals called to shamanism usually experience some sort of "dark night of the soul," often some sort of illness or dis-ease that lasts a prolonged period of time. It is this "illness" that gives rise to the wounded-healer archetype of the shaman. The young shaman goes through some sort of life-threatening sickness that pushes him to the brink of death so that the shaman can cross over to the underworld. It is only then that the shaman can bring back information for the sick or the tribe, and when the shaman heals himself, he then holds the cure to heal those who suffer. The concept of the wounded healer is still primary in modern shamanism.

This is what is sometimes called "Classic Shamanism." The individual is chosen by the spirits, often with no warning, and is not allowed to refuse the gift without suffering illness, insanity, and/or death. Classic Shamanism is nearly always accompanied by a traumatic death-and-rebirth experience, after which the personality is radically changed.

Core Shamanism, on the other hand, is generally entirely voluntary. This is the path I have taken. I chose the path rather than being chosen for it by the spirits. Although a seeker may feel "drawn" to shamanic practices, he is not in danger of illness, insanity, or death for refusing to follow a particular path. He may choose his own human teachers, and he may stop at any time. Although his life may be poorer for it, he will not usually be penalized by the spirits unless he has made specific bargains.

One of the goals I've set to achieve is to bridge shamanism with integral theory, uniting the two into a new, transrational form that is only now beginning to emerge. But emerge from what to what? Using developmental systems theory, we can clearly show how shamanism has unfolded, and continues to unfold, in the developmental context of stages of increasing complexity. These stages are prerational, rational, and transrational. Here's a brief description of shamanism at each of these stages:

- **Prerational shamanism** is the practice of communing with nature and ancestral spirits and deities that are separate from oneself. It is tribal and magical. The shaman makes offerings to these spirits or gods in order to affect or manifest some change in his, or the tribe's, life and to support and honor Gaia by his connection, love, and respect. His dreams are interpreted as the gods, goddesses, or spirits talking to me. This is the home of classic shamanism.

- **Rational shamanism,** sometimes referred to as urban shamanism, views shamanism as metaphor for internal processes and dreams, much like psychotherapists, and looks like "me talking to me." The "unseen" world exists only in our own interiority and the microscopic world. Since we've transcended and included the prerational, we may still have superstitions and mythic beliefs, but spirits are also seen as metaphors. Often, we've lost our connection to Gaia because of our belief in scientific rationalism. Rational shamanism can be either classic or core shamanism.

- **Transrational shamanism** recognizes higher realms of being, of energetic realities and practices, and contains both the prerational and rational so that we may understand our connection to the conscious universe and to science, connecting all in a community of aligned service to the highest good. The "unseen" includes the above as well as the intuited and the experiential "knowing." Dreams are communications from God/Goddess/universal consciousness, often competing with my ego. There is an integration of the connectedness of all things and a return to stewarding the earth as opposed to dominating it. Like rational shamanism, it can be either classic or core.

Not too long ago, I was involved in a discussion about how indigenous spiritual leaders organize (or don't organize) sacred gatherings. By way of background, some indigenous spiritual Native American leaders and shamans had called a meeting and no one showed up. The leaders did not acknowledge a problem and had no interest in doing anything about it.

A few highlights from these leaders' perspectives:

- If it is a sacred gathering, it is not publicized. If someone is to be there, they will find it. Gatherings are made hard to find on purpose.

- Flyers are usually a no-no. It is like if someone calls themselves a medicine man/woman or shaman—run as fast as you can. Only the people can give you that honor.

- It does not matter if there are two thousand people in attendance or one. When an elder speaks, it goes out to the whole universe. Elders are not attached to how many they speak to, only that they can speak.

- They understand that the words "we are all related" are real—that the trees, wind, rocks, and water will carry their words forward. You were fortunate to be one of the ones to experience them firsthand.

- If there are hundreds of seats, they are all filled, even if you cannot see the people.

- Elder gatherings never start on time. It is normal for an elder to be several hours late. They will start when the energy is right.

These indigenous spiritual leaders are clearly coming from the prerational stage. While we need to honor traditional methods and beliefs—because the shaman at any stage is the master of subtle and ecstatic states of consciousness—with later-stage consciousness—the transrational— we see that Spirit can move *through* us, as well as around us. We are the physical manifestation of Spirit, and what we do in the name of Spirit, and in integrity, *is Spirit in action*. We are evolving creatures, and as we evolve, so does our deepening understanding of God and the Universe, as we can only see what our current level of consciousness enables us to see, not beyond, and our perspectives are limited by our current level, or structure of consciousness.

That all states of consciousness, right up to awareness of the nondual, are available to anyone at any level of consciousness has been demonstrated throughout the ages. Shamans, medicine men, spiritual teachers, and ordinary people, have always had ready access to those altered states of consciousness (ever-present, never-changing, the formless), but those altered-state experiences can be interpreted only from an individual's *stage*, or level of consciousness (always changing, evolutionary). What it means to be enlightened in the integral age is very different from what it meant to be enlightened a thousand or two thousand years ago, as newer stages of consciousness had not emerged and simply weren't available. These structures of consciousness explain why so many people have so many different beliefs.

Unless we become aware of ourselves as evolving spiritual creatures, we'll keep doing what we've been doing and getting the results we've been getting. Yes, I agree that the talks of the indigenous spiritual leaders go out through the oneness of everything, into the collective unconscious, what biologist and author Rupert Sheldrake refers to as Morphic Fields,[76] fields of thought created by everything in existence, but I'd prefer that it also goes into as much of the collective consciousness, as well.

Postmodernism must integrate the wisdom and altered-state skills of the shaman and the medicine man, and indigenous teachers must integrate the rational and transrational stages of development. Anything less is only partial enlightenment.

Meta-Shamanism

Going beyond the prerational and rational and into the territory of the transrational leads to the concept of "meta-shamanism,"[77] in which a "meta-shaman moves vertically along the whole Spiral, accessing the

---

76   http://www.sheldrake.org/homepage.html

77   The central theme of meta-shamanism is replacing the traditional images of the axis mundi, around which all shamanic traditions are constructed (often a mountain or a tree, but also a tent pole or sometimes a ladder), with the spiral from Spiral Dynamics.

necessary energies, values, or traits of any given meme[78] as needed to solve the current situation. Within the meme accessed, the meta-shaman is also able to move within the horizontal or vertical orientation of that meme as needed.

The meta-shaman recognizes the entire cosmos as a manifestation of Spirit, the source and destination of the manifest universe. The gods, goddesses, and spirits humans have recognized throughout their history the need to remain alive and valid within each of the v-memes[79] that spawned them.

Meta-shamans are capable of selecting, through a conscious process or intuitively, the meme required at any given time. Within the selected meme, whichever form of consciousness transformation is appropriate to that meme is accessible, whether it's the trance state of the traditional shaman in purple or the nature mysticism of the green meme.[80]

The danger with any traditional practices, whether of a shamanic or traditional religion, is the classic trap of the *pre-trans* fallacy (as first identified by Wilber), in that it mistakes an earlier stage of consciousness (the prerational, or magic) for an advanced stage (the transrational). The use of Wilber's AQAL model and Spiral Dynamics are important additions to shamanism because they place shamanism in a developmental context, helping remove the danger of the *pre-trans* fallacy.[81]

As Wilber points out in his book *Boomeritus*,[82] one of shamanism's great contributions has been providing profound techniques of inducing altered states of a psychic and subtle nature, and that can be a path out of flatland, or "stuck thinking." The trick is to be to be able to take the altered-states technologies of the shaman and fit them into more

---

78   A meme is a cultural concept that is transmitted by repetition in a manner analogous to the biological transmission of genes. As used here, it refers to a developmental level.

79   A value meme, or developmental level based on values

80   Refer back to Spiral Dynamics in Chapter 4.

81   "The *pre-/trans-* fallacy" refers to mistaking earlier-stage consciousness characteristics for later-stage consciousness.

82   Ken Wilber, *Boomeritus* (Boston: Shambhala Publications, 2002).

adequate interpretations. That shamanic *states* exist cannot be denied, but what stage do they get plugged into?

Whatever one's experience is of the shamanic altered-state practice, like all state experiences, they will be interpreted first by the altitude—developmental level—of the shaman, and individually interpreted or reinterpreted by the person experiencing the altered state based on his own development. It is the meta-shaman who must skillfully guide the person having the altered experience through the inner maze of his own consciousness.

In this sense, shamanism is no different from any other path that leads to altered states and transformation. Whether "integral" or meta, shamanism goes beyond traditional therapy and traditional shamanism: during this time of evolutionary unfolding, an integral or meta-shaman may intuitively, or with purpose and intention, use all his tools, all the perspectives, including the integral model, developmental levels, lines, states, and stages, recognizing that the people he is working with can be met where they are. And with use of these skills, including shamanism, he can have a sense of what needs to happen next, healing and opening paths to higher states of consciousness.

Today's integral shaman still walks between the worlds—the exterior world of the ever-changing physical, ordinary, or manifest realm and the interior world of never-changing spirit. Instead of dying himself, today's integral shaman gives people the experience of dying to the old and being reborn to the new. The modern shaman uses ancient knowledge and awareness in the context of our present social and cultural environment. The wisdom and its application are still the same—after all, people still have the same desires and emotions they've always had; only the context of culture is different. Today's shaman still heals the mind, the body, and the spirit. The acts of diagnosing and healing are one and the same for the shaman. In order to grow, shamanism recognizes that we must experience dis-ease and views this dis-ease as an opportunity for growth. We usually don't want to rock the boat, but the shaman wants to rock it, and the integral shaman wants to rock the hell out of it, eventually moving past the temporary phenomenal states into the ever-present self.

Tools of the Integral Shaman

Integral and developmental systems theory aside, the integral shaman recognizes that one of the meanings of the word *shaman* is "one who knows." Shamans have always been recognized as experts in keeping together the multiple codes through which complex belief systems are perpetuated, and the integral shaman understands his or her own culture and acts accordingly. The shaman is known for traversing the *axis mundi* (also cosmic axis, world axis, world pillar, center of the world) and, in religion or mythology, is the connection between heaven and Earth. In Jungian terms, the shaman is the ultimate expression of the Magician archetype, which we'll touch on in a later chapter.

One of the ways shamans traverse the *axis mundi*[83] and enter the spirit world is by effecting a transition of consciousness—entering an altered state or ecstatic trance either by autosuggestion or by the use of entheogens. The methods are diverse, and most of those from plant sources, often psychoactive, are no longer legal—plants like Psilocybin mushrooms, marijuana and cannabis, San Pedro cactus, peyote, ayahuasca, Salvia divinorum, and more. Other methods of creating altered states include dancing, singing, drumming, fire walking, attending sweat lodges, listening to music, embarking on vision quests, and breathing exercises. We'll talk more on the breath and the Shamanic Breathwork Process a little later in this chapter.

As Wilber says, "The profound importance of the shamanic voyage, in any of its versions, was that it was the first great discovery of, and exploration of, the transpersonal domains, and thus many shamanic insights, especially into the psychic realms, remained unsurpassed. In particular, we may note that the shaman, as the first 'psychotherapist,' was the first to discover the extraordinary importance of transpersonal altered states of consciousness for ordinary healing, both physical healing and psychological healing."

The altered-state technologies of the modern shaman create an opening through a magical inner doorway into the innate perennial wisdom lying dormant within each of us. Linda Star Wolf, in her book *Shamanic*

---

83   The world center and/or the connection between heaven and Earth.

Breathwork: Journeying Beyond the Limits of the Self, refers to this inner healer and wisdom-keeper as "the shaman within."[84]

Whether we're talking about Shamanic Breathwork, guided shamanic journeys, Insight Dialogue, meditation practices, or any other methods mentioned, these psychospiritual altered-state technologies and methodologies do, indeed, create some sort of opening that gets our egos out of our way and allows our soul, or spirit, to come forth and assist in our healing and in reawakening our essential self, which is, as Star Wolf says "the very core of our true being."

Combine these essential and ancient altered-state technologies with cutting-edge integral and developmental systems theory, and we have brand new, powerful transpersonal paradigms available to anyone who chooses to use them—the integral shaman. This is the beauty of having all of the wisdom traditions of the planet available to us. The integral shaman no longer travels to other worlds, bringing back information for others, but assists them in their own travels so that they may "walk between the worlds" of the exterior and interior realms of the mind, soul, and universe, opening new visions, new possibilities, and new awarenesses that were previously locked away in their subconscious minds. In other words, it wakes us up.

Shamanic Breathwork: An Integral Process

Shortly after meeting Anyaa McAndrew,[85] the woman who would later become my wife, I was introduced to the Shamanic Breathwork Process. Anyaa—who is a transpersonal psychotherapist and has been a leader in the second-wave feminist movement for some thirty-odd years,—took me through the process while visiting me in Seattle. After just one experience, I was hooked, a common reaction. Here was a powerful process that had the capability of unlocking hidden shadows in one's psyche. It became apparent immediately that one breathwork session was equivalent to six months of intensive psychotherapy. I made a trip out to Isis Cove in early 2007 to attend a week-long Shamanic Breathwork workshop and began a new part of my spiritual journey.

---

84 Rochester, VT: Bear & Company, 2009.
85 http://www.goddessontheloose.com

During that eight-day workshop, I wrote on my blog that, done correctly, this was an integral process, even though the language and the culture are very different from what most "integrally informed" people have experienced. These differences, and the very real possibility of prerational thinking that sometimes gets applied to altered-states work, can have the effect of turning many "integralites" off. This is a mistake, in my opinion. At the very least, no one should make a judgment on the process until he or she has studied it, including having the experience.

I would suggest that with Wilber's book *Integral Spirituality*,[86] the integral model has made a lot of room for accepting other practices into the fold. (This is not to say that the integral approach is not accepting of partial approaches; it obviously is.) As other spiritual practices, religions, and philosophies evolve, there is a natural coming together of viewpoints and perspectives that were not capable of truly coexisting at earlier stages, partly because of awareness and partly because integral has its own language. While the language is cognitive, Spirit doesn't need language—it is experiential, and evolved spiritualism is evolved, with or without the language.

The graphic I created in Figure 9 lays out the Shamanic Breathwork experience in the four quadrants of the integral model. Now, naturally, everything arises through the four quadrants simultaneously, so that in and of itself is not necessarily an indication that a practice, such as Shamanic Breathwork, is of an integral nature.

---

86   http://www.amazon.com/Integral-Spirituality-Startling-Religion-Postmodern/dp/1590303466

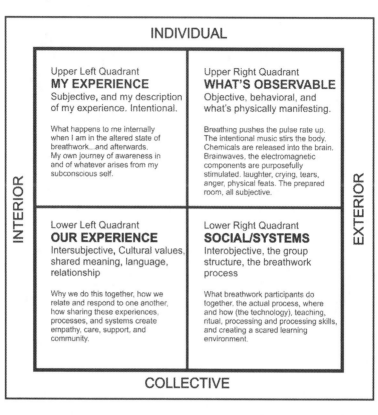

Figure 9

Notice that I did not say, "integrally informed," because, again, the language is different. However, what I think qualifies Shamanic Breathwork as an integral practice is its awareness that all four quadrants are essential to have a "complete," or inclusive, whole and that none of the quadrants are left out of the process. While an individual experience is almost guaranteed, the behavioral, social, and cultural aspects are intentionally included in the practice. The following is from the Shamanic Breathwork Process website:

> The Shamanic Breathwork™ Process is a powerful healing process that inspires individuals to remember and reconnect with their own inner healer. As old wounds and dysfunctional patterns are released and transformed, individuals begin to regain lost soul parts and remember the magic of who they truly are. Empowerment brings wholeness and healing back

into their own lives, to the lives of those they love, and to the world at large.

This process is highly experiential, and the wisdom and healing gained comes from each individual's inner experience. Shamanic Breathwork™ honors and blends the timeless wisdom of ancient traditions with the emerging new paradigm methods of healing and teaching. It functions as the rainbow bridge between these two worlds, honoring the best of both worlds while creating a bridge for body, mind, heart, and spirit.[87]

Shamanic Breathwork provides a safe container in which differentiation becomes integration and can hasten new awareness or even become a new stage. Through death and rebirth, disorienting dilemmas, and the creation of a healthier way to be where you are through horizontal translation or by providing a path for vertical evolution or transformation, Shamanic Breathwork is a process that works.

The Shamanic Breathwork Process differs from others in that it is aimed at awakening the inner shamanic healer in persons going through the process. There is ample support from Shamanic Breathwork facilitators and cojourneyers, who assist during the session in order to ensure a safe journey for the participant and that it is effective.

The process begins by establishing sacred space through various rituals and ceremonies, such as smudging with sage, cedar, and sweet grass while offering prayerful invocations. Individuals lie down on mats and blankets in a darkened room and focus on surrendering to the healer (shaman) within, calling upon that which is most sacred and holy to them, such as guides, power animals, angels, their higher selves, or a higher power. The drumming then begins, which leads into a powerful musical journey varying in length from one to two hours. As the individual uses the power of deep, connected breathing to create a natural, altered, dreamlike state, the ego and its defenses are released and the journey unfolds in a variety of ways.

Each person's shamanic journey is a highly individualized one; no two are ever the same, although I've had breathwork experiences that

---

87   From Venus Rising's website, http://www.shamanicbreathwork.org

were similar to or continuations of earlier ones. Some of the states of consciousness reported by "breathers" range from divine, otherworldly bliss states to the struggle to be released from negative forces in the psyche. Rebirthing is a common occurrence, as is the life review, in which one relives or observes particular lifetime experiences, even including the person's birth. Old patterns of dysfunction may be brought to the surface. Addictions are sometimes healed during this process, and feelings of grief, fear, rage, and anxiety may be released.

Shamanic Breathwork facilitators have undergone this process many times in the course of their training and are loving guides for each participant's journey. The process may require the Shamanic Breathwork facilitator's skills and attention; a variety of psychospiritual tools may be employed to assist the participant. Some of the most commonly used methods are body work, Reiki (energy work), soul return, and extractions. The most powerful healing tool a facilitator can bring to the person breathing is an open and loving heart and mind, along with a willingness to support and travel with the journeyer wherever he or she may need to go. This is the essence of Shamanic Breathwork. Describing the process really does not do it justice. One must experience this powerful shamanic journey and its healing from the inside.

Shadow

One of the most powerful gifts that Shamanic Breathwork can provide is an awareness of shadow. Shadow is sometimes called the deficient, or negative, ego and represents our disowned, despised, and repressed traits. *Shadow* literally means "to obscure the light." Our shadows act out all of the denied emotions and urges we reject—the alcoholic who calls others out and denies his own alcoholism, the sexual prude who winds up acting out his sexual fantasies in secret, the person whose fears and illusions about love turn into codependent behaviors. These are all examples of unresolved issues that go underground as a result of our trying to repress or deny them, and when we do, we act out, manipulate, and project that part of our disowned selves onto others. Hence, the politician who rants against homosexuality and then gets caught coming on to another man in an airport bathroom and the unfulfilled romantic who moves from relationship to relationship looking for that romantic "high," unable to commit are all living in their shadows.

It has been said that one the biggest impediments to our awakening is our shadows—those unidentified parts of ourselves that we are unaware of but that affect us and our lives in so many ways. An unidentified shadow has a tendency to trigger deep, reactive emotions in us. In one of my breathwork sessions, I realized I had deep childhood wounds about which I previously had no clue. After identifying them, I was able to begin a healing process and eventually stop the reactiveness I had been experiencing as my unawakened shadow danced about my unconscious self. Breathwork provided me with the means to "have" my shadow instead of my shadow having me. I still have the issue, but now I have a choice about how I respond to the trigger effect.

The personal experience I cite above is an example of our dark shadows. We can also have shadow in the light realms, what some call our "golden shadows." Our golden shadows show up when we're afraid to step into our bigness—how powerful we truly could be if we weren't fearful of acknowledging that power. One of the shadows I run into occasionally with men is that they're not afraid of failing; they're afraid of succeeding, often because they don't believe in their hearts that they're really worthy of the success they might experience. These men say to themselves—unconsciously, of course—"What if I succeed? Then what do I do?"

At Venus Rising, the parent organization of Shamanic Breathwork, there's a saying: "The light, the dark—no difference." Shadow is shadow, and the shadows of our current stages must be healed in order to move to the next stage without dragging that shadow with us, further compounding the problems of the shadow.

Even our darkest shadows can be amazing gifts! I'm reminded of one man who finally broke through years of hidden childhood abuse to discover that he had an ability to empathize with other abuse victims in a way that someone who had not experienced such abuse could not do. Today he works with other abuse victims in healing those injuries and assisting them in achieving wholeness in their own lives.

How do we identify our shadows? We start by looking at the things that bother us—anger in others, people who are late, people who seem to talk too much. We must look for behaviors that we know we do but that we deny as part of who we are. There are a lot of ways to do this, but breathwork is a fast-track process that allows us to consciously identify, own, and reintegrate the shadow elements of self we all carry—and we are *all* wounded in some way.

Breathwork and Change

Shamanic Breathwork is also stage independent, or developmentally neutral. It provides breathers with what they need at whatever developmental level they currently are.

I have often heard during the course of Shamanic Breathwork preparation with breathers that the realizations gained therein take the participants to new levels of consciousness. Well, yes, *sometimes*. Let me explain.

While sudden insights of previously unknown realizations *can* result in shifts from one level of consciousness to another, we have to first define what we mean by "shifts in consciousness." Are we talking about actual shifts from one level, or stage, of consciousness to another, or are we talking about a simpler shift in *awareness*?

Simply (and it is by no means simple) identifying a shadow does not necessarily result in a shift in stage consciousness (from one permanent structure to another). By far, most experiences resulting from shadow recognition are healing processes. That is, the process identifies a shadow aspect of ourselves that begins the healing needed to transform (vertical, or transformational development) but must begin by the healing contributing to a strong base structure (horizontal, or translative).

The concept of translative (horizontal) development and transformational (vertical) development is critical. People can get a taste (a *state*, or temporary experience) of higher *stages* of consciousness through ecstatic, or altered, *state* experiences like Shamanic Breathwork and "spiritually bypass" their present stage. They think they've moved to a higher level of consciousness when all they're really doing is having a "peak" experience and interpreting that glimpse of higher stages from their present level of consciousness.

What's worse is that if they haven't completed the personal work that needs to be done translatively—that is, horizontal development, the widest and healthiest perspective possible at a particular stage—they tend to disassociate from what they haven't completed, leaving unhealthy aspects of that stage in their psyches that will come back and kick their asses later. It's unavoidable, and it becomes shadow.

It's not until one attains the widest and healthiest perspective at their present stage or translation (also known as *span*) that they're ready to move, in the healthiest manner possible, into the next stage. This is transformation (also known as depth*)*, or vertical development, in which one transcends and includes the previous stage, being able to call on that stage's particular qualities as they are needed. If those qualities aren't healthy, if the work that needs to be done at the present level isn't given the broadest foundation possible to build upon, then pathologies, or shadow, will develop, and we can do ourselves more harm than good.

The Inner Shaman Meditation

Another technique I use with my clients and in the Integral Warrior workshop is guided imagery. Shamanic Breathwork is a self-guided process, aided by music and specific qualities of the breath. Guided imagery, based on Jung's active imagination concept, has many names and associated techniques—visualization, mental imagery, dream interpretation, and more—and is part of the cutting-edge processes used in mind/body/medical procedures. Although it is as old as psychotherapy itself, it's still relatively new in the United States and is experiencing a new wave of respect. A person using guided imagery is relaxed, almost to the point of being in a dream state, but the conscious mind is attuned to listening.

With a skilled facilitator doing the guiding, the individual is focused on the voice of the facilitator, who takes them through a mythic story that begins to stir in the unconscious mind, becoming rich in details, moving and developing, that produce a series of images that eventually unfold into a complete story. Jung said that this process is superior to dreaming in overcoming or defeating the unconscious mind's resistance to allow the buried truth to come to conscious awareness. Like Shamanic Breathwork, guided imagery differs from psychoanalytic cures, which can take months or years.

The inner shaman meditation is a way to get valuable information from our unconscious to our conscious mind and is a meditation for working in and on our inner plane. While in the meditation, we experience and communicate with our inner shaman, who gives us the love, protection, and guidance no one on the outer plane could hope to give us. It's really our unconscious self placed in a witness, or observer, state that brings the information forward. It's simply an aspect of ourselves, and it knows us in a way no other can.

With individuals or groups, I begin with relaxing trance/meditation music in the background. Using my voice at its most hypnotic and relaxed tone, I place the participants at the entrance to a forest trail and begin to take them up a gently sloping path deep into a darkening, thick forest. Coming up to a sheer rock wall, we locate the entrance to a cave. Part of the process here is not to give them too much information about what they're seeing, only what they're doing.

I take them into the cave, following specific steps until they come to a door in the cave. Opening the door, they step out onto a high ledge overlooking a fantastical valley below, where their spirit animal greets them. Again, careful not to give them too much information, the process allows their own imaginations to fill in the gaps. Leading them with statements like, "The valley has trees and foliage in colors and shapes you've never seen before," and "There's a sun overhead but it looks nothing like the sun you're used to seeing," their own minds go to work to create their own images. Even the spirit animal is left for them to create from their own minds, prompted with, "How does your spirit animal arrive?"

The spirit animal then leads them down a path alongside the strange rock walls that surround the valley, past unfamiliar and strange waterfalls, streams, rocks, and trees until they finally find themselves in a place where there is the strangest island of trees they've ever seen, surrounded by a clearing. The spirit animal lies down, indicating that the traveler has arrived at the destination. They walk toward the island of trees, and as they approach, their inner shaman steps out of the trees.

Now, everything up to this point has led to the participants' imaginations firing on all cylinders, and this is where the unconscious really begins to fill in the missing pieces. Asking them to picture what the being looks like that stepped out of the trees, I then have the participants take whoever stepped out through a series of tests that determines if the shaman is truly their inner shaman. If not, we repeat those steps until the participant is satisfied that this is truly their inner shaman. Once satisfied, we can ask them their name and create an agreement with them to give us guidance and knowledge about our lives, our decisions, and our issues, along with as much of an explanation as they can give to our questions.

We can now ask the inner shaman any question about issues that may be affecting our lives—relationship, work, shadow, spirituality—and then wait and listen for them to respond—only listening deeply, not responding—and finally simply mirroring what we've heard. After we've received the information, we thank them, ask them if there's anything else, and if not, let them go.

We then move back to the clearing edge, following our steps back. We pick up our sprit animal, head back up the trail to the ledge, say good-bye, reenter the door, walk back out of the cave and head down the path and out of the forest until we return to the place we started from.

This process takes anywhere from forty-five minutes to an hour, and once traveled, it allows the participant to revisit their inner shaman whenever they'd like to once again speak with them. Again, to reiterate, what we're doing is talking with and accessing the resource of our own subconscious minds, stepping into a witness state where the inner shaman becomes an "other," allowing us to receive information we might not ordinarily obtain.

Shamanism and Sacred Union

Some describe shamanic sacred union as unifying sex, heart, body, and mind. The ultimate description of sacred union is that the universe is permeated by two substances, spirit and matter, and that both flow from the same source, God or universal mind. The unification of spirit and matter reflects God and all apparent existence.

For our purpose of awakening the new masculine, we're going to speak of sacred union as what tantra teacher Deborah Anapol calls "the Sacred Union of Opposites,"[88] the marriage between the masculine and the feminine that is a part of all of us. This is important because until we honor both within our being, we cannot be fully awakened. Anapol describes the difficult play within these two archetypes: "Ancient traditions the world over, which honor the sacred union of male and female and recognize the importance of balancing the masculine and feminine elements within each of us, as well as in the external world, offer us a model for healing. Many of us know intuitively the rightness of finding equilibrium between the energies we call masculine and feminine. We feel the discomfort that arises within us when our internal balance is upset, and we see the unhappiness generated by disequilibrium all over the world. According to Anapol, rarely, if ever, is it understood that the symmetry between feminine and masculine energies, yin and yang, Shakti and Shiva, is the basis for harmony in all of life."

We have all dined at the table of the masculine and feminine, for each is half of who we are in our fullness. If we deny one or the other, we deny ourselves. Our sacred union goal as Integral Warriors is to honor and integrate both the masculine and the feminine within so that we may flow between them at will when they are needed, when it serves, when it's appropriate, or when it just feels good.

In Western culture, the anima and animus—the man's inner feminine and the woman's inner masculine, respectively—were driven underground as a result of bias against acknowledging our androgynous nature. Fortunately, this has begun to shift somewhat in recent years because any effort in keeping the anima and the animus hidden drives them into shadow, and the shadow, as we all know, will not be denied.

For men, balancing and integrating our inner feminine in sacred union

88 http://www.lovewithoutlimits.com/articles/Sacred_Union_of_Opposites.html

with our inner masculine is critical because "the source is feminine … Without the feminine love represented in a reflective way, there is no immortality."[89] Anapol describes the feminine as "the womb from which all emerges." If we don't integrate our internal feminine, if we push it back into darkness, we project it all over the women we come in contact with, especially in intimate relationship, and become defensive, reactive, and isolated. She further explains, "To honor the Feminine, within you and without, take the time to be still, to feel, to savor life. Tune into your body, immerse yourself in water, open your heart, allow the tears come. Meditate, undulate, dance, sing, make love and fill yourself with flowers."

One of the best ways to work on the masculine and feminine energies within is through Shamanic Astrology, which gives us a very helpful map for moving through the cultural and societal changes we have entered. In addition to the larger perspective needed for the immensity of the acceleration and intensity of our interior realm, and the cultural, societal, and survival tools that Shamanic Astrology provides, it's also a way to use and bring forth the archetypal qualities of the masculine and the feminine. These archetypes are called the mediating energies between heaven and earth—a metaphor for interiority and exteriority, the top two quadrants and the bottom two quadrants of the AQAL model. To do this with women, we'd look at their Mars so they can get in touch with their masculine side, and with men we look at their Venus so they can get more in touch with their feminine.

My wife, Anyaa, is a transpersonal psychotherapist and a shamanic astrologer, and because she does most of her work with the psyche, that's the part she's most passionate about—dreaming the dream forward around the cycles of change—through the archetypes of the signs, movement of the planets, and how we're receiving these transmissions and passing them on. Anyaa states, "Those of us who are deeply connected into Shamanic Astrology really feel the ways that the archetypes are evolving as we evolve—they evolve us and we evolve them."

The biggest problem with any type of astrology is the *pre-trans* fallacy— moving the astrology past the prerational, past the rational, and into the

---

89   Sri Babaji Nagaraj, attributed by Deborah Anapol

transrational. According to Daniel Giamario, the creator of Shamanic Astrology, the readings "provide clues within an archetypal and mythical framework creating greater awareness for conscious participation with life purpose and the great mystery." In addition to the prerational—magic and myth, the framework and foundation of all astrology—is added what Wilber refers to as the "as if" framework of the rational level of consciousness and the very high metaphoric or "interpretive" framework of the transrational to events and how they shape and inform our lives.[90]

With Shamanic Astrology, we explore the archetypes of each man's lineage, refining and integrating the dance of his inner feminine and masculine and his best enlightenment and relationship paths. Each man also creates an experiential medicine wheel to acknowledge all of his personal archetypes, deepening his understanding of who he is. Last, each man cocreates a Sacred Marriage ceremony. This is not about telling the future; this is about gaining a deeper understanding of who we are.

Summary of Integral Shamanism

While the roots of shamanism have been long lost, we know it can be traced well back into the Upper Paleolithic era, dating back more than 12,000 years, and surely, they go much further back than that. Some say the first shamans were women and their "magic" was related to blood cycles. Shamanism is said to be the source of both magic and religion. Mircea Eliade[91] called shamanism "an archaic technique of ecstasy." It's only been in the last fifty years or so that shamanism has moved from its limited research status with anthropologists and psychoanalysts to new popularity that is being devoured by those seeking ancient wisdom and a sense of belonging in a seemingly disconnected world that demonstrates very little wisdom. Phil Hine explains the revitalization shamanism:

---

90   mp3.rapidlibrary.com/index.php?q=ken+wilber+divination+astrology+and+the+pre+trans+ fallacy

91   Mircea Eliade is one of the most influential scholars of religion of the twentieth century and one of the world's foremost interpreters of religious symbolism and myth.

Shamanism shows a remarkable survival, and there are many examples of shamans coexisting with other religious or magical systems in a given culture. Most of the world's healers are shamans, for example. As societies evolve into more complex forms than that of the hunter-gatherer, the roles that the shaman fulfils [are] taken up by others. From shamanism arises theatre, religion, magic, art, dance, music and perhaps even writing and language. Traces of shamanism remain, in folklore, customs and myth—deference to those who can manipulate the hidden forces of the world as tricksters and healers. Westerners are increasingly turning to shamanism in a search to revitalize and reintegrate themselves into a worldview which is beyond that offered by our culture. [92]

Today, we can find businessmen attending workshops that include fire walking, sweat lodges, drumming, singing, fasting, and physical feats of endurance. Writers like Carlos Castenada, Lynn Andrews, and my friend, community mate, and teacher Linda Star Wolf have made shamanism accessible and popular.

Just as cultures and societies evolve and become more complex, so does shamanism. That's reflected in integral and meta-shamanism, where the combination of ancient wisdom, knowledge within, the ability to create community, and ways of being integrated with science and rational thought allow us to reconnect with ourselves, making adapting to the world around us much easier.

We now know that the demons and devils that the prerational shaman sought to exorcise are but elements of our own being, our interior selves. We are the modern-day demon, and our inability to wake up is our curse. Traditional shamanism has given us techniques for addressing the unseen world that exists *outside* of us. Urban contemporary shamanism has provided us with techniques for addressing the unseen world that exist *within* us, and integral shamanism offers techniques and practices for addressing an unseen world that exists both inside and outside of us simultaneously.

---

92   Phil Hine, *Walking Between the Worlds: Techniques of Modern Shamanism*, Volume One, 1986.

As a master of subtle states of consciousness, which reveal the energetic patterns that manifest as waking reality—science, medicine, interpersonal relationships, business, politics, the arts, and so on—the integral shaman's path is one of service. That service, at the transrational level, includes all states—gross, subtle, causal, and nondual—all structures, all quadrants, and all types, and it helps others discover something about their true nature, that unchanging, ever-present self.

In the Integral Warrior process, integral shamanism assists with the work that needs to be done by the mature masculine—perhaps not fearlessly, but once enough work is done, fearlessness can also become a trait, a way of being, an embodiment. And a fearless man who lives in freedom epitomizes the Integral Warrior.

CHAPTER 8: MASCULINE ARCHETYPES: THE HIDDEN FORCES AT WORK IN OUR PSYCHES

Some of us disown our sexual instincts, while some of us are very identified with our sexual impulses and are trashy sluts. —A joke showing disowned archetypes expressing themselves in a socially acceptable way

ALL OF US, MALE or female, exhibit an either masculine or feminine essence—that is, who we are. While the terms *male* and *female* represent gender qualities and very much play a role in who we are, men and women can each have either masculine or feminine essences. When applied to the masculine or feminine, the term *essence* is really all about how we manifest and live our daily lives, regardless of our gender.

Gender is a physical description of who we are and, as we have all seen in the last few years, can be changed, which is often related to the disconnect between a person's gender and his or her sexual essence. Our essence goes to the very core of who we are and can range in an individual from very masculine to very feminine, including a multitude of combinations of the two.

The concept of the archetype is derived from the repeated observation that, for instance, "the myths and fairy-tales of world literature contain definite motifs which crop up everywhere. We meet these same motifs in the fantasies, dreams, deliria, and delusions of individuals living today."[93]

Archetypes, as described by Jung and later wonderfully expanded upon by Robert Moore and Douglas Gillette, can be either feminine—the Anima—or masculine—the Animus—and we each carry both. We each come from a man and a woman, so it should not be shocking that we carry those aspects within us. Each essence, masculine or feminine, also carries its archetypes. In the Jungian model, there are four major archetypes: the masculine versions are the King, Warrior, Lover, and Magician, and the feminine, or Goddess, versions are the Queen, Warrioress or Amazon, Lover or Aphrodite, and the Wise Woman or Crone. We could go much deeper into the feminine archetypes, but that is beyond the scope of this book. I do, however, have a recommended reading for those who want to learn more about the feminine archetypes.[94]

Also, rather than doing a whole teaching on each of the masculine archetypes in this format, I'm going to leave that to Moore and Gillette and their book *King, Warrior, Magician, Lover,* for a comprehensive overview of the archetypes, and their book series, which includes *The Warrior Within, The Magician Within*, and so on, for those of you who really want to explore each of the masculine archetypes in depth. All are excellent and highly recommended.

I'm going to do a brief overview of each of the archetypes and the roles that the other archetypes play in keeping each balanced and healthy. That these archetypes are part of our psyches is unassailable. Whether they are healthy or not is an entirely different matter. Let's start with the Warrior.

The Warrior

The Warrior is probably the best known of all of the archetypes. Men

---

93   C. G. Jung, *Memories, Dreams, Reflections* (New York: Pantheon Books, 1973), p. 392.
94   Recommended reading: C. G. Jung, *Aspects of the Feminine* (Princeton University Press, 1982).

throughout time have been called to be warriors, usually in the form of a soldier, and usually against their will in service under conscription as cannon fodder. As an archetype, the Warrior is highly focused and driven to achieve. He is result and goal oriented. Warriors take charge and assert themselves whenever they can, tackling challenges head on. The Warrior is also very disciplined and is supposedly not afraid to take big risks to get whatever he wants, although I challenge the assumption of no fear, as I tend to think that Warriors do experience fear but are capable of overcoming it. Without fear, there is no courage; without fear, we would just be automatons.

Historically, many men have become warriors because it was the only path available to them to get what they wanted, even including a wife and a family. Men who succeeded in those big risks were rewarded, and the men who did not succeed, or did not take risks, did not get to leave their seed to future generations. In the book *Is There Anything Good about Men?*, sociologist Dr. Roy F. Baumeister says,

> When it comes to humans, the simple fact of the matter is that a woman can only get pregnant by one man (at a time) while one man can impregnate multiple women. This is why a woman's eggs, and her womb, have always been much more valuable than a man's seed.

> So in primitive times, in the days before widespread monogamy, the odds that a woman would become a mother were very good. She did not have to do much apart from making herself desirable and wooing the best possible mate. The chances were, even if she did not do much at all, she would get an offer. Her main concern was landing a father for her children that could provide food, protection, and good genes.

> On the other hand, the odds that a man would become a father were not good. The alpha males of the tribe, who were the most desirable to the women because of their good genes and high status, could sire children with numerous partners, shutting out the less attractive and successful men from fathering any children at all.

So men had to do something, the bigger the better, to raise their status and thus improve their chances of reproducing. Women could be relatively sure that they would have at least one child, so it did not make sense for them to give up this sure thing to sally forth on an adventure that might win wealth and glory, but might just as well result in complete failure or death. Regardless of what they did, and what kinds of worldly success they found, they would never have more than a dozen or so children. But it did make sense for a man to take big risks to win wealth and glory and elevate himself above his rivals. If he did nothing, the chances were that he would have *no children*. If he gambled on a risky venture, he might die or fail, but he might make it big, so big he might even father 50 or 100 children (or as many as Genghis Khan!).

All of this is to say that the men of the past were *highly motivated* to take on large challenges that would give them a chance to gain wealth and glory and thus prove themselves as men of high status—alpha males who would be rewarded with numerous chances to sire progeny.

So is this a good look at one of the ways the Warrior—and men—developed and why we do the things we do even today? Aggressive men became fathers, and passive men did not. How much of our literature, stories, mythology, and movies revolve around this theme of the hero taking risks and getting the woman and the rewards?

Today, we're in a new world: masculine energy today is largely equated with patriarchy, as many—especially women—are uncomfortable with that energy, never noticing the irony that those who would cut off or deny the Warrior fall under the power of the archetype. And because men and women today have a tendency to repress the Warrior archetype, the repression goes underground and into shadow. That repression shows up in men playing "warrior games" in gangs, corporations, politics, movies, and almost everything to do with men.

Warriors find success because of their drive, determination, and ambition. They are natural goal setters who like going after results. Many traditional entrepreneurs and business leaders have dominant warrior archetypes. Warriors are also very much at home in the red, orange, and yellow value memes of Spiral Dynamics.[95]

Pitfalls of the Warrior

Warriors can easily fall into the trap of pursuing the signs of success (money, power, fame, glory) in a way that is not fulfilling to them. They may find themselves completely out of balance, having sacrificed parts of their lives to achieve their results. Because Warriors tend to value achievement over fulfillment, they often focus so much on the destination that they fail to enjoy the journey.

Once they lock on a target, Warriors pursue it feverishly and persistently until they achieve their goal, even if they have to make sacrifices along the way. Their persistence tends to be inflexible and uncompromising, and it often easily turns into stubbornness and leads them into trouble if their current strategy is inferior or not working as intended.

The ability of the Warrior to focus can be a blessing and a curse. I've come to believe that the feminine multitasks much better than the masculine. Many times, while I'm in the middle of really concentrating on something, I've found that Anyaa has been speaking to me and that I've only just at that moment become aware of it. I've learned to do one of two things: either say, "I'm right in the middle of something. Can you give me a moment or two?" or to completely stop what I'm doing and refocus on her with all the presence I can muster. If I try to keep doing what I was doing and listening to her at the same time, I'm not being fair to her or to me because I can't be fully present.

The active shadow of the Warrior is the sadist, and the passive shadow of the Warrior is the masochist. Some examples of the Warrior's active shadow are the fighter pilot in *The Great Santini,* played by Robert Duvall, who runs his family like a mini Marine Corps; Darth Vader in *Star Wars*; avenging gods in situations like the Wrath of Shiva or Yahweh's fiery destruction of civilizations with floods and plagues. The active shadow is connected to the immature hero/warrior—the boy

---

95   See Chapter 5, p. 28.

playing a man but who is unsure of his legitimate power so he has to keep proving himself no matter what the consequences.

The active shadow of the Warrior shows up in our own lives through compulsory personality disorders and work- and rage-aholics, and he is obsessive about rules, organization, perfection, and control. They are inflexible, rigid, and stubborn; he cannot delegate; and he can be miserly, as with hoarding money.

The passive shadow of the Warrior avoids confrontation and responsibility, allows himself to be pushed around, and suppresses his anger, becoming sarcastic and pessimistic and blaming others. He has negative attitudes, fears intimacy, and can be overly sensitive, quick to point out the shortcomings of others. The passive shadow of the Warrior shows up as Bridget Fonda in *Single White Female* and as Walter Matthau in *The Odd Couple*.

For the vast majority of us, it's not *if* we are possessed by one or more shadow aspects but *how*. While we all have a dominant archetype, the balanced Warrior accesses the King, Magician, and Lover archetypes. We'll take a look at that after we talk about the other archetypes.

There are a plethora of practices and exercises that can be used to enhance the positive aspects of your Warrior, including meditation, exercise (yoga, weights, walking, swimming), free-form writing, and journaling or blogging. As with all the archetypes, I also suggest that you spend some time thinking about who the major Warrior influences were in your life, both positive and negative, and how those influences challenge or support your mature Warrior. Close your eyes and, using the practice of ruthlessness, the sword of truth, and the compassion of the knife, cut away the illusions you might have. If you need to forgive yourself first, do it. When you experience the presence of Spirit within you, open your eyes. When you finish, spend some time writing and reflecting on your experience—what you've learned and what you still need to do. A word of caution: don't do this exercise with any of the archetypes until you've read Moore and Gillette's book about that archetype and have a clear understanding of it.

Once you've done the work around your shadows and integrated them, take some time to do the first of what I call the four initiations with the Integral Warrior initiation.

The First of Four Initiations: The Warrior

At the end of each archetype segment in the Integral Warrior workshop, there's a final element to each of the four primary archetypes. That is the initiation oath. Each man who chooses this path must write his own initiation oath and create a ceremony around it. This is easier and more powerful if done in a group but is not absolutely necessary

The Integral Warrior initiation is the death of the victim/victimizer and the patriarchal warrior of old. A man must die a shamanic death to the old before he can be reborn as the integral, shamanic, or spiritual Warrior.

In this ritual death, a man must give up having power over others and accept the role of knowing himself and using whatever power he has for the benefit of his loved ones, his community, and the world.

The Warrior initiation is not an achievement. It is a gift from that which cannot be named. It cannot be earned like a degree, bought, won, or displayed like a trophy. A man can choose whether to accept it gracefully and with courage; to be dragged through it screaming, kicking, and crying; or to ignore it and continue dressing the wounds that will not heal.

No one can initiate a man in this process but himself. A guide only points to an open door to another world. It is each man's responsibility to return from that world to this one with the gift of self and the self's relationship to the world. Through this gift, each man takes responsibility for his thoughts and actions with focus, commitment, courage, and passion.

We are living in a time of great change on our planet. The conflict now is between three mythic belief systems: the technological-economic myth of progress and growth, authoritarian and patriarchal religion, and the emerging spiritual worldview that we are all connected and life is sacred. The challenge we have is determining how we live a spiritual life in the material world.

Once you've done the work described, write your own initiation statement. Keep it to about two minutes or less in length. Choose your words carefully. Again, it would be best if you were to be witnessed and honored by other men.

> **Example:** "I claim the courage to be conscious of what I have ignored by owning my shadows; by being in integrity with what I say and do; by modeling healthy masculinity; and by being of service to my family, my community, and the planet with my mission and my purpose."

The best way to do this is with a group of men who can witness your oath and who share your purpose and mission around integrating the archetypes. I've done this with men who have then burned their oaths over a fire, wadded them up and buried them in a secret place, floated them off down a river, and even eaten them! The perfect place is in the workshop through a self-initiated ritual designed by you and the other men, but that may not be possible. You may have to do it on your own, and I urge you, even under those circumstances, to treat it as the sacred ceremony that it, and you, deserve.

Here are a couple of Warrior initiation statements from men who have completed that initiation:

> I embrace the integral warrior by being true to myself, loving and nurturing to others, and by taking responsibility for my actions. I bring my shadow warrior into the light so we can walk hand in hand in a powerful, compassionate way. Aho! —John Shanton Wilcox, Winston-Salem, NC

> No longer afraid to confront and own who I truly am at my core, I now unashamedly and proudly integrate and reveal the true masculine nature of my conscious warrior. Confident and strong, and yet, humbled, I call forth the Warrior Archetype in service to the Big Picture King and the world, tempered by the knowledge of the magician, and the compassion and appreciation for beauty of the lover. I own the shadow aspects of my warrior,

thereby allowing me to choose and take responsibility for my actions, instead of living in the reactiveness of the old warrior, the soldier. —Name withheld by request

I fully accept my birthright as an integral warrior. I will use my warrior to attack life and live it to its fullest. I will model the new warrior masculinity to my family and all those I encounter. I reject the traditional warrior who only seeks to dominate with no regard to consequences. As the new warrior I will be bold and deliberate with my actions, all the while aware of how my actions impact the world. The knowledge of my mortality is what will allow my warrior to truly live. —Bobby DuPlantier, New Orleans

Do this also with each of the other three archetypes.

The Lover

An understanding of the four major Jungian archetypes quickly points out how important balance is between them, their relationships to one another, and how this balance, or lack of balance, affects our own behaviors. By understanding and accessing archetypal behaviors, we are able to step back, relegate our own behaviors into third-person terms, and observe and witness how these behaviors influence and play out in our lives. The Integral Warrior dives deep into each of the archetypes.

For instance, the Lover archetype, one of the four major archetypes, is probably the most misunderstood of all of them. The Lover, accessed properly, gives us a sense of meaning in our lives. This sense of meaning is, I believe, the essence of spirituality, no matter where one might fall on a developmental evolutionary scale or map. Traditionally, every man who was married was assumed to hold the Lover archetype, but men who identified with the lover were usually artists, musicians, or thespians and were looked at as being feminine.

The idealist and the dreamer are two examples of the Lover, deeply immersed and connected to the energy of the universe. The Lover is also playful, sensual, tuned into his physical environment, passionate and compassionate, joyous and creative, living in every moment.

The Lover appreciates and surrounds himself with beauty, including art, music, relationships, food, his home, and his very life, treating it all as art.

The masculine Lover keeps the other masculine energies human, loving, and related, helping the King, Warrior, and Magician to harmonize with one another and preventing detachment in them. Each of the other archetypes needs the Lover to keep them from becoming sadistic.

The Lover needs the other archetypes, as well:

- The King defines limits and boundaries for the Lover, bringing structure and preventing the Lover from becoming an addict, one of the Lover's shadow sides.

- The Warrior helps the Lover act decisively so that the Lover can detach from immobilizing sensuality and prevents fixation and obsession, an easy place for the Lover to go, appreciating beauty as he does. The Lover, without the discipline of the Warrior, runs the risk of sliding into addiction.

- The Magician keeps the Lover's emotions in check, brings objective perspectives, and helps the Lover see the bigger picture and the reality beneath the seeming.

Accessing the Lover

If you want to develop your Lover archetype to its fullest possible expression, express appreciation of beauty; open your eyes and your heart to the beauty that surrounds you in everyday life; take dance lessons; do sensual practices; turn sex into art. Listen to music that moves you and move with the music. Make music and art a "practice of presence." Learn to play an instrument. Sing.

Most of all, do what you love—or do more of what you love. Learn to love what you do, learn to live with what you do, or, if it comes to this, leave what you do.

Develop your compassion and creativity quotients. In *The Hidden*

Spirituality of Men, Matthew Fox says, "All of the spiritual traditions of the world agree that compassion is the ultimate expression of our better selves, of human morality." And we must always remember: Beauty is immortal, but beautiful things are not.

The integrated Lover initiation marks the transition from a purely masculine or feminine perspective to the sacred union of the Divine Feminine and the Divine Masculine. As with the Warrior archetype and the death of the victim/victimizer and the patriarchy of old, a man must be willing to die a shamanic death to the old masculine-versus-feminine construct before he can be reborn as the fully integrated, or shamanic, Lover.

In this ritual death, a man must give up suppressing his feelings and creative instincts and face his fears of being consumed and emasculated, as well as his tendency to be possessed by the Lover, which can manifest itself as an addictive personality. He must be willing to step away from too much or too little emotion (the drama king or the stoic) into a life of passion and devotion.

Your Oath as an Integrated Lover

Please write your own initiation statement, keeping it to about two minutes or less in length. Choose your words carefully. Ideally, you will be witnessed and honored by other men who take this journey with you.

> **Example**: "I claim the courage to overcome the emotional challenges of life, to be compassionate, empathetic, and passionate. I am not afraid to tell the truth, even in defiance of the Warrior and the King. I claim the right to hold an open heart without fear and to embody the integrated Lover, freely moving between the masculine and the feminine as is needed in the present moment, the *now*. I am the epitome of sensuality, see the world in all its splendor, and seek to experience beauty and unity in my daily life by making each moment a 'work of art.' I have stopped 'performing' and have relaxed into just 'being,' embodying the Lover in all its passion."

The following are actual initiation statements, or declarations of intention, of men who have completed the Lover initiation:

> "I will not be afraid to let the feminine shine, and I will not feel emasculated because of it. I'm not responsible for others' lack of understanding and will not carry that burden any longer. I embrace my sensitivity while rejecting the stoic and drama that has been my lover's shadow for too long.
>
> My sensitivity is not weakness; in fact, it strengthens me, by integrating my true dynamic self. Love believes in me and I surrender. To be true to the rhythm of my soul and let it shine in any time of darkness, or light for that matter, in order to let the universe hear my song. My song of love." —Robert James McCarroll Sr.
>
> "I, Chuck, the Green Man, in this moment accept the courage to open my heart to all of life's gifts and abundance. I bravely step into my shadow to release the pieces that no longer serve me. And through my healing, I honor their role in my life. I am released from the shadow's prison of judgment and fear and into complete freedom in an effort to fully embody my inner Lover. I vow to honor my inner lover by intentionally connecting to the Divine through my creativity, passion, awareness and sensuality in everyday life. I am creating a more fulfilling, rewarding and abundant life by honoring my God-given gifts from this day forward. Aho." —Chuck Wilhide, the Green Man

The Magician

There are a lot of different types of magicians. The Magician is the initiate of secret knowledge, and, unlike the Warrior, who struggles to overcome great challenges, the Magician believes in infinite potentials and possibilities. Rather than struggling against the current, the Magician flows with it. Throughout history, medicine men, wizards, shamans, witch doctors, *brujos*, scientists, teachers, doctors, and inventors have been connected to the archetypal pattern of the Magician.

The Magician does not seek to find answers from someone else but goes within to access inner truths. He wastes no time or energy on fear-based thinking, knowing that we have a cocreative nature and that our thoughts shape our reality. The Magician chooses to live beyond the ordinary and realizes that the opportunity to enter the realm of the miraculous lies in every choice we make. He transmutes muck into gold and the negative into the positive. Technology, at whatever level of development or stage, is the Magician's specialty.

When the energy of the Magician manifests, one experiences what Joseph Campbell refers to as "the Call," and the Magician's quest and his journey in sacred time begin, finally ending with "the return." The Call comes to us as life changes or through trauma, and we experience the "dark night of the soul." Hopefully, guided by another Magician—a therapist, elder, or shaman—we come to a good end.

Celeste Adams offers the following thoughts about the Magician archetype:

> As we become more aware of the Magician archetype and the possibilities it holds for us, we begin to come into greater contact with it in the people that we meet, in the articles and books that we read, in television, and in films. This interplay between our own personal experiences and events in the external world is an example of our cocreative nature, which implies that psyche and matter interact and are not separate and independent from each other.
>
> Now, during this crucial time in earth's history, when we are dealing with the very real threat of nuclear warfare and bioterrorism, the Magician knows the importance of focusing on the best outcome, and doesn't allow personal energies to be diminished and dissipated by fear.
>
> As we cultivate the Magician archetype, we change the direction of our own life and influence the course of our planet's evolution.[96]

This is the modern magician's task and challenge.

---

96 http://www.spiritofmaat.com/archive/jan2/magician.htm#fn

The Integrated Magician

Initiation means "beginning." This beginning can be the initiation *of* something or an initiation *into* something. If you want to fully integrate the Magician archetype, you must be initiated into magic, the known and the unknown. Initiation into magic occurs at the moment you make an explicit commitment to fulfill two obligations—to realize to the utmost your individual potential and to serve other people with everything you have. These two themes express what Thomas Berry describes as "the Great Work." By being here in a circle of men, and even by reading this book, you are already doing both of these things—if you dare, magic puts you in the fast lane to awareness of this fact and thereby makes you better at what you do.

As with the other archetypes, a man must be willing to die a shamanic death to the old before he can be reborn as the fully integrated, or Shamanic, Priest/Magician. In this ritual death, a man must give up his detachment, isolation, passivity, and fear of not being "enough." He must willingly, consciously, and completely step into wholeness and empowerment.

Please write your own initiation statement, keeping it to about two minutes or less in length. Choose your words carefully. You will be witnessed and honored by the other men.

> **Example:** "I claim the archetype of the Magician, the Shamanic Priest, and the embodiment of the new masculine. I claim my two-million-year-old intellectual birthright, my access to the magician potentials within, and announce my embodied involvement and commitment to myself and to all humankind. I claim my highest ideals and vision of what is possible through the magic I have access to through the Magician archetype. I will not surrender my mind to others. I vow to continue to learn, grow, expand, and increase my own awareness, modeling for others as I go, and I claim and assume my full role as a human elder for an inclusive human community."

The following are actual Magician oaths and affirmations:

> I embrace the integrated magician, the shaman within. I claim

access to my magical powers and vow to use those powers in a good way and not allow them to possess me and drive me compulsively into isolation. I commit myself to the continuing study of what it means to be a light being in physical form. I will honor all teachings while taking only those that serve highest good and that best serve all of humankind. I will stand true to myself and not be swayed by others who do not have my best interest in mind. I will be a beacon of light, a model for others as I assume my full role as a human ritual elder for an inclusive human community. Aho! —John Shanton Wilcox, Winston-Salem, NC

I am the Magician and the Shamanic Priest and I vow to utilize that powerful aspect of my masculine being for the betterment of my global tribe. I will continually refine those magical powers and apply them at every opportunity to increase awareness in others to better understand the magical powers they have. In doing so I will strive to raise the level of consciousness of the collective—beyond the corporate world and the obsolete and destructive patriarchal rulers of this world. My intent will be to guide where and when I can to demonstrate that we are all one with each other and that it is only in one unified spirit we will be able to transition into a better place. It is with Love, Compassion, Integrity and Honor I enter into this contract and invite the universe to present the opportunities for me to give back. I now welcome those opportunities and will not make excuses to pass them up. It is my time! —Anonymous

The King

Like the Queen, the King is an archetype of major proportions. The King represents the pinnacle of temporal male power and authority. He also manifests spiritual and generative qualities. He brings the courage of the Warrior, the passion of the Lover, and the wisdom of the Magician to his kingdom and the world. The King archetype is the domain of material manifestation, family, "kingdom" (your sphere of life influence including your relationship to individuals and physical locations: home, neighborhood, community, city, state, country, world), and material wealth and abundance. When the King is in balance, his kingdom—whatever it might be—prospers, and when the King is out of balance, the kingdom suffers. The King plays the central role of order and blessing, benevolence and fertility, strength and balance.

Both benevolence and cruelty in their extreme expressions are associated with this archetype. The King maintains the same characteristics on an individual level, whether his kingdom is a corporation, community, or family. The need to rule and exert control over a kingdom is key to this archetype.

Here's what being with a man who is in the fullness of the King archetype feels like:

- He is concerned with the well-being and easeful happiness of those he engages with.

- He is a stabilizing and calming influence in all circumstances. By his balance and "potency" (strength, effectiveness), others are comforted and influenced to imitate his example.

- His demeanor is "seasoned." He carries wisdom, not adolescent impulsiveness.

- He is complex, with multiple aspects that comprise his unique expression of the divine.

- He displays transpersonal selflessness, like a kind father.

- He is an agent of the divine, having reverence for all life.

- He is benevolent, evenhanded, calm, strong, caring, present, and passionate.

- He is settled in the knowledge that everything is as it should be, everything changes, and there is no lack or anything to genuinely fear.

The Shadow of the King

The shadows of the King are the tyrant, or the active shadow of the king, and the weakling, the passive shadow of the King.

Manifestations of the tyrant include bullying, aggressive and negative behaviors, and resentment. Andrew Collinson gives a good explanation of the tyrant and the weakling:

> The tyrant thinks he knows it all and will not listen to anyone else. In the end, he is either overthrown or just ignored. This will come at a terrible price not just for the person concerned but, sometimes, in the case of the great dictators, whole countries suffer. The tyrant has no conception of service to those under his care, so his fall is inevitable. He has never "followed his bliss" and so cannot bear to see anyone else follow theirs.
>
> The polar opposite of the tyrant is the weakling. This is the man who is moody, listless. He would rather go and sulk in the corner than stand up for what he believes in. He may go off and lie on a beach in Bali for years, thinking he is being really cool but in reality not having a clue what his life is about. Whilst not as destructive as the tyrant, he is still of no use to the world as he is giving nothing.
>
> Put pressure on a weakling, however, and he will jump to the polar opposite of the tyrant, screaming abuse at all those around him. The weakling and the tyrant can be very close buddies.
>
> If you are out of touch with your King archetype, look at those around you, as a denied archetype is always projected upon someone else. So who dominates you? You will find, I am sure, that you give them the blame for everything that is not right in your life. Take back your power and restore your King to throne.[97]

---

97   Andrew Collinson, "The Shadow King—When the King Archetype Goes Wrong," October 17, 2009. http://EzineArticles.com/3107391

The Integrated King Initiation

The King is all about integration and aspiration. The King integrates the other archetypes, steps into the fullness of all of the archetypes, and manifests spiritual or generative qualities. He brings the courage of the Warrior, the passion of the Lover, and the wisdom of the Magician to the world. All energy flows from the King, he is the source. When his life is in balance, his kingdom—the world—prospers. When he is out of balance, he and the world suffer.

What do you need to claim or allow to die to step into your fullness as the King? As with the other archetypes, a man must be willing to die a shamanic death to the old before he can be reborn as the fully integrated King. In this ritual death, a man must give up his tyrant or his weakling, the shadow aspects of the king. He must willingly, consciously, and completely step into wholeness and empowerment.

Please take some time to seriously consider your own initiation statement. Choose your words carefully, as if you were being witnessed and honored by other men.

> **Example:** "I claim the archetype of the King and the individual and collective authority that comes with the fullness and benevolence of the King. I do this with purpose and determination, knowing that taking ownership and responsibility for my own balance and manifestation increases my consciousness and thereby raises the consciousness of everyone on the planet to some degree. I vow to continue working on my passive and active shadows, my physical (Warrior), emotional (Lover), intellectual (Magician), and Spiritual (King) aspects of reality. I take responsibility for all of my actions and no longer need to create grace but expect and demand grace from myself and others. Last, I recognize the King inherent in all men and assume the mantle of model and teacher to the best of my ability."

And, again, the following are samples of the declaration of intention in the form of initiation statements written by men who have completed the process:

> This is my formal declaration to be what I have feared, and

now surrender to. I willingly step into the archetype of the King, along with the acknowledgment and authority that comes with acute discernment encompassed within, along with the perspective of a loving ruler which embodies the positive elements consisting of a passionate lover, a reluctant warrior, and a conservative magician, all of which enable me to balance and manifest completeness while recognizing the shadow elements within, thus gaining control and taking the power from the dark. I will use these abilities as a loving soul that manifests the new integrated masculine within me. —Robert James McCarroll Sr., Whittier, NC

I embrace the fullness of the king. I take responsibility for my actions as I honor the wisdom of my magician, the strength of my warrior and the compassion of my lover. I will make the best decisions that I feel are right for me, my loved ones and for my community. I will be a model of strength, stability and balance for others to see. I am the ruler of my inner kingdom, radiating light outward for all to draw comfort from. I vow to myself, my loved ones and to all who are influenced by me to be a compassionate, strong, knowledgeable and wise king. Aho! —John Shanton Wilcox, Winston-Salem, NC

"I, King Chuck the GreenMan, boldly claim and embody the King archetype! I call on my inner King and use my leadership to bring balance and guidance to my inner Warrior, Magician and Lover. In this moment as an integrated King, I banish the tyrant king and the weak king, for they no longer serve me. I am now able to move more fully into my power with grace and ease, and be a shining example, to all who are in my presence, of spiritual leadership. It is through my King that I accept responsibility for my part in affecting my sphere of influence and creation of my reality. I choose to proactively live my life to my fullest expression without reservation or apprehension. Being present in the moment without fear or judgment will be my main mode of operation. I now am stepping into life with focus and purpose to be the teacher King to all of those needing a helping hand, guidance, love and compassion. I rule my kingdom with peace, right action and my inner connection to the Divine. Through my intent to proactively have communion with Source, I am able to effectively and efficiently create a life of ease and great abundance. It is my responsibility to then share the completeness of my life with others so they can know the happiness within me! Aho. —Chuck Wilhide, the Green Man

Balancing the Archetypes

What an amazing time we live in! For the first time in history, we have access to all of the wisdom traditions, philosophies, and religions of the world through prerational, rational, and transrational cultures. Remarkably, we also, for the first time ever, have an opportunity to fully integrate each of these archetypes into our being. The following is from Chapter 1 of this book:

> "Men that go through the Integral Warrior men's process complete four initiations, calling in and claiming their king, their warrior, their lover, and their magician, so that none of them dominates the others, but rather, all of them balance one another in perfect masculine harmony."

> "This is a remarkable achievement in that, historically, most cultures only affirmed one or two parts of a man—usually the Warrior and sometimes the Magician. Very few men got to be initiated as Lovers, and even fewer as Kings.

> Our job today, as Integral Warriors and shamanic priests, is much more difficult because we must affirm, educate, and validate all four archetypes, letting them simmer and grow together to create a full man. Now we need enlightened and transformed Magicians, Lovers of life and beauty, and strong nonviolent Warriors to produce truly big-picture men—or Kings." [98]

While it is obviously more difficult to integrate all of the archetypes, it is also an evolutionary challenge of increasing complexity. With the

---

98   Richard Rohr, *Adam's Return*, 2004.

opportunity to integrate all of the archetypes comes the opportunity to find balance in our lives that we could not previously attain, a balance we talked about earlier in this chapter in the section about the Lover. Some other aspects of this balance include the following:

- The Warrior helps keep the King in balance by being willing to speak out and offer other viewpoints, as opposed to the blind obeisance of a soldier.

- A Magician, without the compassion of the Lover on board, creates genetically modified foods, nuclear weapons, and deadly microorganisms.

- A Warrior, without the compassion of the Lover, the big-picture awareness of the King, and the knowledge and intellectual capacity of the Magician, becomes a killer.

- And again, the Lover, without the discipline of the Warrior, becomes an addict.

Combining and integrating all of the archetypal aspects of who we are allows for an "archetypal shift." Theoretical biologist Rupert Sheldrake's theory of morphogenetic fields—presented in *A New Science of Life: The Hypothesis of Formative Causation* (1981)—points toward the development and emergence of new archetypes. It means that when enough people accept a new pattern of behavior, the scale eventually tilts, becoming the accepted way of doing things. It is the "hundredth monkey" hypothesis in action.

The dominant archetypes in our own lives are based upon cultural influences as well as our own unique history. Historically, our culture defined the hero as the archetypal Warrior who lives life battling a series of challenges, but a shift seems to be occurring. The Magician appears to be emerging as an archetype that may play a central role in the third millennium. And while the Magician may soon replace the Warrior as our culture's most important figure, the Warrior will remains a much-needed archetype in the coming times.

In the meantime, some of the myths carried by the archetypes that affect our lives will also need to go away.

- One is the myth that the earth has an infinite wealth of resources. We cannot afford to continue to lose 120 species of life and 200,000 acres of rain forest every day.

- The Genesis myth of man being given dominion over all things has created a world that is out of balance and in disharmony. Humans are not the crown of creation but exist as one of the jewels in that crown. We need to look at and perhaps embrace myths from older cultures, where all life is considered sacred.

- The myth of original sin says it was a woman who tempted a man to eat from the tree of knowledge. Fruit of this poisoned tree is that, today, right-wing fundamentalist men of many religions—including Christianity and Islam—are controlling the lives of women because they consider them to be inferior and evil. In Afghanistan, women have experienced extreme segregation and oppression. Fundamentalist groups in Pakistan and Kashmir have thrown acid in the faces of unveiled women. In general, long-term Warriors have a tendency to see women as a corrupting force.

When we understand the myths that are guiding our lives and our cultures, we can begin to change them. We can free ourselves from undesirable myths and create new ones to guide us through the new millennium.

That puts the concept of archetypes in a developmental or evolutionary model. Some of the challenge for men today are to become aware of the shadow aspects of the archetypes and to integrate their healthy aspects so that we may consciously influence the direction and course of our planet's, and our, evolution. That is the Integral Warrior's big-picture task and challenge.

Chapter 9: What Do I Need to Work On? The Psychology of Spirituality or the Spirituality of Psychology?

Just because I'm in overwhelm doesn't mean I'm a bad person.
—Gary Stamper

ONE OF THE MANY ways to apply integral theory in the Integral Warrior workshop is through the usage of an integral psychograph. An integral psychograph looks at an individual's lines of development, one of the five aspects in the integral model. As we learned earlier, the others are the four quadrants, types, stages, and states. These are different kinds, or types, of intelligences, as found in Howard Gardner's work on multiple intelligences.[99] There is no one measurement of intelligence; rather, we are made up of many different kinds of intelligences.

The integral psychograph is based on the idea that we have multiple and distinct interior capacities and that they tend to develop in lines at various rates of complexity and depth.

The ones we're most concerned with for an integral psychograph are these:

1. **Cognitive**: Thinking clearly and rationally; having reasoning capabilities; solving; being able to sort things out, make

---

99   http://www.tecweb.org/styles/gardner.html

plans, and see multiple perspectives. The cognitive sets the stage for all of the other intelligences.

2. **Interpersonal**: Interaction with others. People who are highly developed here tend to be extroverts. Seen in how we notice distinction among others—in particular, contrasts in their moods, temperaments, motivations, and intentions.

3. **Psychosexual:** Development of the individual's sexuality as affected by biological, cultural, and emotional influences from prenatal life onward throughout life.

4. **Emotional**: Four types of abilities—perceiving, using, understanding, and managing. Describes the ability, capacity, and skill to identify, assess, manage and control the emotions of one's self, of others, and of groups.

5. **Moral/ethical/values**: The capacity to understand right from wrong; it means to have strong ethical convictions and to act on them so that one behaves in the right and honorable way.

6. **Kinesthetic or physical**: Control of one's bodily motions and capacity to handle objects skillfully; are generally good at physical activities such as sports or dance. They may enjoy acting or performing, and in general they are good at building and making things.

7. **Aesthetic/artistic**: May be music, art, writing, love of beauty. The ability to produce, express, communicate, and appreciate in a compelling way the inner, spiritual, natural, and cultural realities and meanings. (This can include aspects of verbal, musical, and spatial intelligences.)

8. **Spiritual**: Sometimes called the ultimate intelligence and the guide for all the other intelligences, it is the soul's intelligence, the intelligence of the deep self. It is the intelligence with which we ask fundamental questions and with which we reframe our answers.

9. **Empathy/compassion**: Those with high empathetic intelligence do well at commiserating, "reading" others, making themselves likable as well as persuading and manipulating. The emotionally intelligent know what reactions their own actions will produce in others before they act.

States and Stages and the Integral Psychograph

The nine "intelligences" listed at the top of Figure 10 are but a few of the lines of development in the integral model. So why are these important in our development? To be fully evolving, we need not only to feel and have state (or temporary) experiences (as in altered-state work) but also to know how and where we need to evolve, which aids us in our rapid transition to later stages (permanent structures) of consciousness. This realization allows us to consciously participate in our own evolution. To do this fully, we must consider all five of the aspects of the integral model, including lines of development.

INTEGRAL PSYCHOGRAPH WORKSHEET

NAME _____ DATE _____

1 2 3 4 5 6 7 8	< LEVEL or STAGE
	Cognitive intelligence
	Interpersonal intelligence
	Psychosexual intelligence
	Emotional intelligence
	Moral/values/ethical intelligence
	Kinesthetic/physical intelligence
	Aesthetic/artistic intelligence
	Spiritual intelligence
	Empathetic/compassion intelligence
	Giving feedback
	Interviewing
	Listening
	Analyzing an interpersonal situation
	Synthesizing information to form an hypothesis
	Identifying emotions in self
	Identifying emotions in others
	Leading an interpersonal development skill process
	Reading nonverbal cues in self
	Reading nonverbal cues in others
	Identifying reasons for and types of conflict
	Diagnosing reasons for ineffective communication
	Appreciation & understanding of human diversity
	Intuition
	Sense of humor about self
	Judgment about when to seek assistance & feedback
	Willingness to consider unsolicited feedback
	Capacity to hear the true message behind what's being said
	Capacity to inspire trust
	Self-confidence
	Facilitation of meetings
	Effective participation in groups
	Capacity to read an audience

Figure 10: Integral Psychograph

To use this sheet, take, at a minimum, the first nine categories. On a scale from 1 to 8, representing the first eight levels of development from the Spiral Dynamics model in Chapter 5, mark how developed you think you are in each of those lines, or categories. To check yourself, consult with a trusted friend and ask him or her to score you, as well. Discuss the two sets of scores and why those scores might be different.

You don't have to be a concert pianist or a successful artist to rate high in the aesthetic/artistic intelligence lines. You only have to have an appreciation of the beauty contained within, and the higher the appreciation, the higher your score. The same goes for each of the other intelligences. Also note that the different lines that make up a psychograph will be more relevant in some contexts and less in others. For example, the lines most useful for a psychotherapy context are not necessarily the same ones most useful for a life or executive coaching context.

For a deeper look into other intelligences, or lines of development, go ahead and complete the entire chart. You might be amazed at what you learn about yourself. For instance, if you want to be a workshop facilitator or therapist but your interpersonal skills are lacking, you might want to improve on that.

When you're done, there are other capacities where you might need to improve. For instance, what if you're really smart (high on the cognitive intelligence line) but are really lacking in the emotional intelligence category? You could be a really smart, angry guy! Consider that it might be better to see where you need work so that you can begin to balance who you are. The advantage of using this tool is 1) knowing your own strengths and weaknesses so that you can more easily and effectively navigate life and all that comes with it, and 2) the chart shows how close your consciousness is to being whole with everything. While this is an evolving tool with many complexities that continue to emerge, it's also a valuable tool in determining what we need to work on.

The integral psychograph is another way to flesh out the integral map. Like Shamanic Breathwork, it also helps us take a look at who we truly are. Again, we're concerned with balance, in making sure we have all the necessary pieces to do the work we want to do in the world, so we do the cognitive work that prepares us for a deeper understanding of the experiential elements (like meditation, journeying, or Shamanic Breathwork), which, together, help us shift to new stages of consciousness by allowing us to interpret both normal and altered-state experiences from the highest perspective possible.

Last, don't assume that because we're really powerful and highly developed in some lines that we're also highly developed in the others. We've seen too many politicians, spiritual teachers, and public figures crash and burn because of their arrogance around their undeveloped lines. The integral psychograph helps us understand our strengths and our weaknesses so that we may become fuller, more rounded, and holistic.

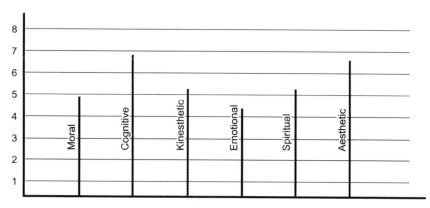

Figure 11: Integral Psychograph from *Integral Spirituality* by Ken Wilber. What do you need to work on and why?

The Shamanic Breathwork Process is another way to discover what you might want to work on. As explained in Chapter 7, Shamanic Breathwork allows our egos to get out of the way of what our souls want to bring forth from our subconscious. This can point to places of grief, where we get angry, where we hurt, and all sorts of unfinished business that stems from the childhood wounding we all received from our primary caretakers.

Meditation, particularly loving-kindness meditation, is another way to discover what we need to work on. In meditation, we simply observe what comes up for us. Just by sitting and doing nothing, we are doing a tremendous amount. Each meditation session is a journey meant to help us more deeply understand the basic truth of who we are. It can also bring about compelling insights and certain kinds of deep healing.

Meditation also has its limitations. Meditations don't do it all but are an important part of a complex path of opening and healing. From my own experience, not only can meditation open the doors to being more spiritual, but it can help identify major areas of difficulty in life. In my case, this happened because, while mediation wouldn't touch or heal things such as loneliness, intimate relationships, childhood wounds, or patterns of fear, it did help me to see what they were. Sometimes mediation can be used to hide and avoid the problematic parts of ourselves through blissed-out states of spiritual bypassing.[100]

Jack Kornfield says we need to look at our whole life and ask ourselves: "Where am I awake, and what am I avoiding? Do I use my practice to hide? In what areas am I conscious, and where am I fearful, caught, or unfree?"

So, with meditation, we just sit and observe, just to see what is happening.

Last, I also suggest that men consider taking on an Integral Life Practice. ILP is a map for physical health, emotional balance, mental clarity, and spiritual awakening that consists of "spiritual cross training," that can radically accelerate all of your dimensions and lines. ILP is integral theory in practice. It includes shadow, body, mind, and spirit modules in an integrated practice that will help you grow and develop to your fullest capacities. Toward developing an ILP, I recommend the book *Integral Life Practice* by Ken Wilber, Terry Patten, Adam Leonard, and Marco Morelli.[101] Combine this practice with an integral psychograph,[102] and you have a powerhouse of transformation that creates balance and fullness. You don't need to become a master of all of the lines; you just need to be aware of them to create that balance. It's as easy as bringing truth, beauty, and goodness into your life.

---

100   Robert Augustus Masters, *Spiritual Bypassing*, North Atlantic Books, 2010

101   Boston and London: Integral Books, 2008.

102   Wilber et al., Integral Life Practice, 2008, p. 83.

Chapter 10: The Missing Link for Boys and Men: Initiation and Ritual

Ritual is necessary for us to know anything. —Ken Kesey

Deep, unspeakable suffering may well be called a baptism, a regeneration, the initiation into a new state. —Ira Gershwin

To discover the heart is the greatest initiation. —Inayat Khan

I AM CONSTANTLY AMAZED at how many initiations I go through—at how many we all go through, mostly without realizing it. There are the everyday initiations that come to us without planning, and then there are the more formal initiations that serve a specific purpose or goal.

Sufi Master Inayat Khna elaborates:

There are different kinds of initiation that souls experience. One is natural initiation. A kind of natural unfoldment for which the soul cannot give any cause or reason, comes to a soul, although no effort or attempt has been made by that soul to experience it. Sometimes this initiation comes after great illness, pain, or suffering. It comes as an opening up of the horizon, it comes as a flash of light, and in a moment the world seems transformed. It is not that the world has changed; it is that that person has become tuned to a different pitch. He begins to think differently, feel differently, see and act differently; his whole condition begins to change. One might say of him that from that moment he begins to live. It may come as a vision, as a dream, as a phenomenon—in any of these forms; one cannot determine the manner in which it will manifest. —Inayat Khna, Sufi Master

You only have to reread the introduction to this book to understand why male initiation is so desperately needed today. Initiation is a rite-of-passage ceremony marking an entrance or acceptance into a group or society.[103] It could also be a formal admission to adulthood in a community or one of its formal components. In an extended sense it can also signify a transformation in which the initiate is "reborn" into a new role. Examples of initiation ceremonies might include religious or spiritual ceremonies, trade unions, tribal initiations, puberty rites, secret society inductions, baptism, rites of passage, marriage, death, bar mitzvahs, graduation, debutante balls, circumcision, communion, vision quests, baptism by fire, Boy Scouts membership, and so on. In most cultures, however, the original initiation was only the first of an informal, continuing initiation process. Once a boy is initiated into manhood, he is, required to prove himself over and over. As Dr. Roy Baumeister puts it, "A woman is entitled to respect until and unless she does something to lose it. A man is not entitled to respect until and unless he does something to gain it … The man must repeatedly achieve: obtain, surpass, conquer … Insecurity is part of being a man, an essential part of the male role in society. Manhood is never secure: It must be claimed via public actions, risky things seen and validated by other people—and it can be lost."[104]

Reasons for and Functions of Initiation

Joseph Campbell states that it takes a "hero's journey" for boys to become men and for men to revitalize themselves within the context of our twenty-first century culture and immediate life circumstances. Postmodern man, by and large, has been lulled to sleep, and it both is and isn't their fault. Men either have succumbed to the pursuit of things or have gotten stuck in overfeminization rather than learning to feel,

103   http://en.wikipedia.org/wiki/Initiation
104   Roy F. Baumeister, *Is There Anything Good About Men?: How Cultures Flourish by Exploiting Men* (Oxford University Press, 2010).

followed by owning those feelings and reclaiming their masculinity. Both the pursuit of objects and the overfeminization of men are at fault. As we've just learned, as long as we live in the manifest realm, a hero's journey is never over. We are constantly having to reprove ourselves. David Deida offers this explanation: "One misunderstanding is that if you do the right thing, then life's storms will stop. If you do the right thing, the storms actually get bigger. This is because they know they can't blow you down like they used to, and now it's going to take a lot more energy to find out if you are conscious."

We must face life's realities as they, not we, wish them to be. We are the ones who bring meaning to our lives. We create purpose and passion as we make our own way on our individual paths. In this manner, following our bliss is not narcissistic or indulgent but essential for living our lives authentically, courageously, and with wholeness and presence. We then inspire others through our living embodiment—a radiance that comes from within and can then be transmitted to the world.

As it stands today, we are only now beginning to reclaim and rediscover the importance of rites of passage and initiation—processes that can help boys grow into men and men into spiritually mature elders and that can return us to our hearts as we still stand strong in our masculine essences.

In his book *Adam's Return: The Five Promises of Male Initiation*, Franciscan priest Richard Rohr unearths the complexities of male spiritual maturation and helps us to understand the importance of male initiation rights in both culture and the church. Rohr says,

> Initiation rites might well be described as a brilliant form of that "certain difficult repentance" and the "realization of life's mistake." This is at the core of classic initiation—and psychological genius besides. Most scholars and historians of initiation seem to agree that the stages of initiation rituals are something like this. It has been called the "monomyth of the hero" because the pattern is so universal.[105]

---

105 Joseph Campbell, *The Hero with a Thousand Faces* (Pantheon Books, 1949).

1) Separation from business as usual old roles, feminine affirmation, etc.

2) This moves the initiate, hopefully, into a "threshold space."

3) Here a numinous encounter is possible, desired, and required.

4) Now the initiate returns to his community with a new identity and a gift for the community, although his primary gift is the man he has become.

This is exactly what the Integral Warrior process is designed to. By bringing men together—either on multiple weekends spaced about a month apart or in online learning classrooms—the process separates us from our usual surroundings and roles, dropping us directly into the company of men where, for many of us, for the first time—and because of the safe context—are given permission to communicate with each other at a much deeper level than we are used to.

Then, through meditation, movement, cognitive work, the exploration of shadow, and energy work, we step into a new way of being, of relaxing authentically, which in turn allows us and our hearts to soften, let go, and open. This is the threshold space that allows *something* to happen.

The following are what Rohr calls the five essential messages of initiation:[106]

1. Life is hard.

2. You are not that important.

3. Your life is not about you.

4. You are not in control.

5. You are going to die.

These five massages are the quintessential elements of Deida's concept

---

106   Richard Rohr, *Adam's Return*, 2004.

of third-stage masculine. When a man can relax into and accept these messages, he is truly free. The entire Integral Warrior process can be summed up as the opportunity to integrate and embody these messages of initiation. When men get these points, what usually happens is an awakening to their original selves and their original faces at the deepest level, a realization of who they really are, an encounter with the Divine, Spirit, or God—and themselves. It is here that men discover what they are here to do, their "purpose," their mission in life, and what their deepest gifts are. This "numinous encounter" is the transformation, what wakes them up, and their new passion in life.

Men then return to their partners, their children, their loved ones, and their communities with a renewed sense of who they are, and in their emergence ceremony, which we'll get to in the final chapter, they proclaim their new identities and their gifts to the world. But as Rohr points out, the primary gift to his loved ones and the world is the man he has become.

The five essential messages may, upon first hearing them, sound negative, but it is about giving up our ego-based preconceived notions of who we think we are in order to discover our true nature. If we're holding onto our egos, the message is threatening and negative. The initiations and the message are about separation from codependency, from our limited self-image, from the autonomous ego, and from the insecurities of boyhood. They can feel like a giant shove into the responsibilities of manhood, especially to Western man.

That we've become so identified and addicted to these illusions completely explains why we're where we are: fundamental silliness on the conservative right—the red and blue memes of Spiral Dynamics— and the secular arrogance of the liberal left—the orange and green memes of Spiral Dynamics. What might we have become and what might the world look like today if men had continued to experientially learn these five essential messages and if a critical mass or a cultural elite had experienced this enduring wisdom?

As Rohr says, "We have some major surgery to do." The shadow is the way in and the way out. Of all the work we can do for ourselves, none is more important than shadow work and no work is more powerful than the ritual death and rebirth encountered in Shamanic Breathwork.[107]

- Ritual death can lead to conquest of the fear of real death.

- Ritual death can be used for transformation and rebirth.

- Initiation's function is to reveal the deep meaning of existence to the new generations and to help them assume the responsibility of truly being men and hence of participating in culture.

- It reveals a world open to the transhuman, a world that, in our philosophical terminology, we should call transcendental.

- It also leads the initiated to open to spiritual values and the mystical vocation limited to the few who are destined to participate in a more intense religious experience than is accessible to the rest of the community.

Today, the collective unconscious resides in conformist thinking, and wisdom figures are relegated to the unheard edges. The first lesson of initiation is to teach men not to run from pain, "and in fact, not to get rid of any pain until he had first learned its lessons."[108] We can do much better. The way up is first of all the way down. [109]

The four initiations of the Integral Warrior process, anchored by intense shadow work, provide the major surgery needed for men—and the masculine—to find, develop, and bring their greatest gifts to the world, whether it's creating something as amazing as a new way to help others see what they could not see before or as simple (?) as living an impeccable life of integrity.

Initiation and ritual are miles away, philosophically and spiritually, from hazing. The following is a description of hazing from StopHazing.org:

---

107   See Chapter 8, Integral Shamanism, Shamanic Breathwork.

108   Richard Rohr, *Adam's Return,* 2004.

109   Ibid. Author's note: I owe a huge debt of gratitude to Richard Rohr. This chapter would not exist if not for his book *Adam's Return.*

133

"Hazing" refers to any activity expected of someone joining a group (or to maintain full status in a group) that humiliates, degrades or risks emotional and/or physical harm, regardless of the person's willingness to participate. In years past, hazing practices were typically considered harmless pranks or comical antics associated with young men in college fraternities. Today we know that hazing extends far beyond college fraternities and is experienced by boys/men and girls/women in school groups, university organizations, athletic teams, military, and other social and professional organizations, causing emotional and physical harm and even death. Hazing practices are shaped by power dynamics operating in a group and/or organization within a particular cultural context. As such, hazing also reflects societal norms and expectations around gender, and masculinity, in particular.

Men who have had hazing experiences are often deeply triggered when they come up against initiation, and even "joining" certain types of groups can be frightening. The initiation process of the New Warrior Training Weekend from the Mankind Project is an example of an initiation that can be triggering for some men. My own experiences with hazing led me to develop a serious dislike of that part of the weekend as a man who has experienced hazing as brutal, hierarchal, abusive, humiliating, and hazardous—and that was just a college fraternity initiation. So when I come up against men who were deeply triggered by the process, I understand.

Elizabeth J. Allan, PhD, points out that "how men and women are taught to live in the world affects patterns of violence, abuse and other behaviors involved in hazing practices. Regardless of race and socio-economic status, accounts of hazing incidents among boys and men often include tests of physical endurance, forced/coerced alcohol consumption, paddling, and other forms of physical assaults/beatings. A common rationale in support of hazing is that it is a "tradition" necessary to "weed out" those unworthy of membership and reveals an emphasis on hypermasculinity, as the more boys and men are fearful of being labeled as weak, the more likely they are to participate in hazing activities that can be dangerous or even life-threatening.[110]

---

110   http://www.stophazing.org.

A lack of initiation creates two debilitating factors: 1) the dominance of boy psychology—the stunted masculine, fixated at immature levels— which is all around us and is easy to point out. This "boy psychology" shows up as abusive and violent acting-out behaviors against each other, women, cultures, and the planet. And 2) the cultural and social organization of patriarchy that has ruled much of the planet for thousands of years. Robert Moore points out, "Patriarchy, in our view, is an attack on masculinity in its fullness as well as femininity in its fullness. Those caught up in the structures and dynamics of patriarchy seek to dominate not only women but men as well. Patriarchy is based on fear—the boy's fear, the immature masculine's fear—of women, to be sure, but also fear of men. Boys fear women. They also fear real men."[111]

In his last book,[112] Campbell called for a worldwide awakening to a new kind of initiation that would become a rallying point for a deepened human sense of maturity and responsibility. We desperately need to call an end to the reign of *The Lord of the Flies* "apocalyptic fantasy of the end of the world in a final display of infantile rage." If the new masculine can take on the task and responsibility of their initiation and those of young men moving from boyhood into mature manhood as seriously as our shamanic and tribal ancestors did, then maybe we can move into new ways of being and beginnings instead of the beginnings of the end of our species.

Of course, all of this depends on how well and how fast we can step into facing our own immaturities.

What is certain is that initiated men will provide liberating, empowering, and healing ritual leadership for their families, their sons, and their world. Initiated men will steward their shamanic potential for the earth community, shape-shifting themselves, young men, and our world into higher levels of being and maturity.

---

111   http://www.creationsmagazine.com/articles/C84/Moore.html
112   Joseph Campbell, *The Inner Reaches of Outer Space* (Novato, CA: Joseph Campbell Foundation, 1986).

Chapter 11: Sacred Activism: Shape-Shifting Your World

The dream is everything—the waking dream as well as the sleeping dream, our visions of who we are, where we want to go. It affects all aspects of our lives, whether we admit it or not. Once you understand this, then you're in a position to start moving energy around. That's when shapeshifting begins to happen. —Viejo Itza quoted in *Shape Shifting*, by John Perkins

A spirituality that is only private and self-absorbed, one devoid of an authentic political and social consciousness, does little to halt the suicidal juggernaut of history. On the other hand, an activism that is not purified by profound spiritual and psychological self-awareness and rooted in divine truth, wisdom, and compassion will only perpetuate the problem it is trying to solve, however righteous its intentions. When, however, the deepest and most grounded spiritual vision is married to a practical and pragmatic drive to transform all existing political, economic, and social institutions, a holy force—the power of wisdom and love in action—is born. This force I define as Sacred Activism. —Andrew Harvey

Dr. Susan Corso—writing for the *Huffington Post*—called Andrew Harvey "one of the bad boys of the modern spiritual path." "Bless the man," she wrote. "He's almost always ahead of the curve. His book, *The Hope: A Guide to Sacred Activism*, is no exception. Sometimes, taking on changing the world can seem overwhelming, and we just want to give up. Mr. Harvey does not see it that way."

Most activists are addicted to doing, and many spiritual people are just as addicted to being. Sacred Activism is a transforming force of do-be-do-be-do compassion in action that is born of a fusion of deep spiritual knowledge, courage, love, and passion, with wise radical action in the world. The large-scale practice of sacred activism can become an essential force for preserving and healing the planet and its inhabitants. The Institute for Sacred Activism^{TM,SM} is an international nonprofit organization focused on inviting concerned people to take up the challenge of our contemporary crises in order to become inspired, effective, and practical agents of institutional and systematic change, in order to create peace and sustainability.

Dr. Corso also says, "*The Hope* demands nothing less than the true integration of matter and spirit, masculine and feminine, self and others. It is a masterful panorama of how to get from the world as it is to a world as it could be."

Why Is Sacred Activism Crucial for Our Future?

The economic, political, and spiritual global crisis that we currently find ourselves in is a call to action. It is more than an opportunity for us to understand the realities around us and to rally together to do something different. It's a necessity if we are to survive and to birth the new human. We have before us the possibility of using this current crisis to empower ourselves and others to actually get the planet to work. Embracing an uncertain future, we need to support new emerging leaders who are inspired, courageous, and effective in their rising up because the old ones cannot take just where we need to go. We need to renew the energy of people who are burnt out and apathetic in institutions and corporations. If we point individuals to an inner compass that renews their passion, there is hope for real solutions and inspired creativity. All that we need is already there in the currency of people, and it only needs to be tapped into.

Neither contemporary spiritual seekers nor activists have been connected to a vision of action that is inspiring, hopeful, and rooted in deep spiritual wisdom and compassion. Some spiritual seekers, for instance, use spiritual knowledge as a subtle way of dissociating from, or spiritually by-passing, hands-on, realistic, social, economic, and political engagement in the world, thereby ensuring that the world and its people will be abandoned in their hour of extreme need. The postmodern monk must come out of his or her sanctuary and be engaged.

Activists—the warriors, if you will—-are prone to complete exhaustion, to burning out and debilitating and divisive rage and are often cut off from the healing and transforming wisdom of the spiritual traditions and the simple techniques, prayers, and practices that could sustain, inspire, and nourish them in their heroic endeavors. Sacred activism embodies an integral, or holistic, approach that combines all the spiritual and wisdom traditions that have come before and provides a clear way forward.

We have seen that in the very heart of the chaos of the modern crisis, an extraordinary lineage has arisen of ordinary people who have fused these wisdom traditions and deep spiritual knowledge, experience, and practice with wise, incessant action for justice and peace. Having emerged against all odds, they accomplished the unimaginable.

The vision of sacred activism is dedicated to honoring and continuing the tremendous work of extraordinary people such as Mahatma Gandhi, Martin Luther King Jr., the Dalai Lama, Nelson Mandela, Rosa Parks, and Desmond Tutu. Each of these individuals rose up to meet the challenges of his or her time with great spiritual grace and integrated inner contemplation with decisive action. The work of Paul Ray and Paul Hawken reveals to us that there is in our contemporary world an arising of different groups of concerned people anxious for change. Sacred activism provides these people with a system of thought and traditional wisdom practices to help support the kind of transformative change that is necessary for the world to be preserved.

Do you remember the seventies bumper sticker that said, "Fighting for Peace is like Fucking for Chastity"? Andrew Harvey points out that the most visible world activists are often "fighting for peace," an "ironic position that doesn't really match the roots of our planetary problems," and suggests ten things that can begin to align yourself with the power of sacred activism.

1. Be grateful.

2. Ask yourself: what's sacred to me?

3. Cultivate forgiveness.

4. Read sacred words.

5. Pray or ask to align with love.

6. Develop a spiritual practice.

7. Make a small gesture.

8. Take a baby step for world hunger.

9. Reach into your community.

10. Choose a cause.

11. (Because the number "11" is a sacred number) Extend compassion.

The first six invite you into a deep spiritual connection, and the next four can help you express the compassion and joy that the first six awaken in you.

Being grateful: This and keeping an open heart, even when I want to close down, is my primary practice. No matter what's going on in our lives, there's always something we can find to feel gratitude about. It might be that first waking moment, something as simple as a cup of coffee, or the sound of children laughing. Harvey recommends that we carry a small notebook with us and occasionally write about the things we notice that we feel gratitude about. At the end of the month, review them all by reading them out loud, slowly, to yourself. You'll be amazed at how blessed you'll feel. It can also awaken in you a passion for life and a hunger to protect and preserve it.

What's sacred to me? Sit down, and without too much thinking, jot down something that feels sacred to you. As I write this, my word today is *relationship*. Spend the day thinking about your word and how it fits into the sacred within your life. You'll find that this inspires you and gives your day even more meaning as you reflect on your deepest values and joy.

Cultivate forgiveness: Stop for a moment and reflect on someone who has hurt or betrayed you. Close your eyes and imagine that person standing in front of you, bathed in the light from your open heart. With humble sincerity, see him or her happy and smiling. Perhaps using loving-kindness or Tonglen meditation, send the person compassion, light, and love. You'll be amazed at how it comes back to you.

Read sacred words: There are so many texts that can inspire us. I'm reminded of Marianne Williamson's "Illuminati" or the poems of Rumi. When we read and dive into the words of these mystics, we literally touch the face of God.

Pray or ask to align with love: When the text you have chosen starts to light up your spirit, pray a short prayer that aligns you with the "pure deep love" that is longing to use you as its instrument in the world. Here are four from Harvey that he says he uses "at odd moments" throughout his day:

- Lord, let me live to be truly useful.

- Beloved, make me strong enough to do Your will.

- Divine Mother, fill me with your passion of compassion so that I can do your work tirelessly.

- For as long as space exists and sentient beings remain, may I too remain to dispel the misery of the world.

If none of these inspire you or reflect your beliefs, make up your own spontaneously and say it ten times with passion in the core of your heart.

Develop a spiritual practice: Make a commitment to start one now. Close your eyes, take a deep breath, and just watch your thoughts come and go for three minutes. So simple, right? Now spend three minutes— just three minutes—to allow your mind to sit silently. What did you find? Not as simple, is it? That's why it's called "practice." If you can't do this or find it boring, Harvey recommends a visualization given to him by a great Tibetan master: "Imagine that love and compassionate action has transformed you into a large brilliant diamond that radiates diamond-white light. Send that light to all the four directions, praying, with whatever words you choose, that all sentient beings everywhere be happy, well, and protected."

Start doing it at different times in your day—"anytime, anywhere." You will soon learn that it has the power to bring you to your most compassionate self and your desire and hunger to help others.

Make a small gesture: Commit to easing the pain and struggle of others. Ask what they need and then help them to ease their pain and suffering in whatever way you can to make their burden a little lighter. Do it in gratitude and love.

Take a baby step for world hunger: Commit to skipping a meal once in a while and sending a check for what you would have spent to a reputable organization that is working to relieve world hunger. Never forget that a couple of billion people live on this planet on less than a dollar a day.

Reach into your community: At every moment, there are people and families all around you who are struggling and suffering. Make a commitment to find out who they are and what they might need. Find some friends who are willing to make a commitment to help supply these families with what they need. There are more of them than you might imagine. You will, by your actions, activate the compassionate and King heart of your community.

Choose a cause: Don't wait to make a commitment, even if you are also struggling, to tithe 5 to 10 percent of what you make to something you believe in, a cause of your choice. Choose it as a way to demonstrate your gratitude for what you do have, your abundance, and give it no matter what happens, give it freely, and give it with joy. Harvey says responding now will immediately empower you.

And one last suggestion because 11 is a sacred number and the number of the hexagram "tai" in the "I Ching" that means "peace."

Extend compassion: Make a commitment to always have some spare change in your pocket to give something to one of the many thousands of homeless people in our streets. Harvey tells the story of how, outside a temple in South India, there was a long line of desolate-looking beggars and among them a very old woman, dressed in a ragged and filthy sari, with no shoes. He gave her what he had on him—about a dollar. "I watched in amazement as she walked unsteadily over to the nearest food-stand, bought herself a handful of chapatis, broke them carefully in two, and shared them with a dog as emaciated as she was," Harvey says. "If we all knew what that penniless old woman knew, many of the millions of children who die of starvation every year would be alive today."

Sacred Activism and the Integral Warrior

Following Joseph Campbell's well-known quotation "Follow your bliss," Harvey presents an inspired variation: "Follow your heartbreak," asking each reader, "What breaks your heart?" There's your work. To do that requires a major awakening and a transformation called shape-shifting. The Integral Warrior begins to experience the inner joy, outer effectiveness, and profound transformation of this force and literally "shape-shifts" his life and his circumstances to fit that life and those circumstances.

As Robert Kennedy said in 1966, so eloquently and accurately, "Each time a person stands up for an ideal, or acts to improve the lot of others, or strikes out against injustice, he or she sends forth a tiny ripple of hope. And crossing each other from a million different centers of energy and daring, those ripples build a current that can sweep down the mightiest walls of oppression and resistance."

I've been a "shape-shifter" all my life—I just didn't know it. I moved into my life as a professional singer in clubs, Las Vegas, and even concert halls for ten years after graduating from college with a BA in graphic design eventually left that to reinvent myself as a business owner and designer once again, found my spiritual path in the 1990s, "discovered" Ken Wilber and integral philosophy in early 2001, and finally moved to North Carolina in 2007, where I married my beloved Anyaa and obtained my master's and a PhD in shamanic psychospiritual studies, studying and writing the thesis that has become this book. Each change, each chapter of my life was a shape-shift into something new, something more powerful, all building on one another, all leading up to discovering my ultimate passion and whatever gifts I can bring to the world.

Sacred activism is a more integral and complete way to be both spiritual and an activist. It's no longer enough for us to disengage from the world and meditate from our temples or on top of a mountain. Sacred activism is about, to borrow from Gandhi, being the change we want to see in the world. Again, the words of Andrew Harvey: "Sacred Activism is the fusion of the two noblest fires of the human heart; the fire of the mystic's passion for God with the fire of the activist's passion for justice. It embraces all religions and all spiritual paths to celebrate the essential Oneness of divine reality and work with the mother force of love and wisdom in action to create a healed, just, luminous, compassionate one-world. I believe it to be nothing less than the birthing force of the one divine and so the key, not only to human survival but to our necessary evolutionary transformation."

So how does one become a sacred activist? Harvey says it's by making a steady commitment to combine five interlinked forms of service—to the Divine, to yourself as an instrument of the Divine, to all sentient beings in your life, and to your local and your global community. Harvey continues:

> For most sacred activists the greatest challenge is to look after the body. The Christian mystic Father Bede Griffiths once said to me, "Imagine that God is a great musician and that you are a flute He wants to play the most glorious music on. If the stops of your flute are filled with mud, how can the music that is meant to be played through you sound at all?" By removing the mud from the "stops" of your sacred instrument—yourself—with prayer, inspiration, and diet, exercise, and rest, you can allow your body to renew itself and live in balance.

> If you honor the need to serve yourself as an instrument of the Divine, you will discover, over time, that you will have far more compassionate and healthy energy to give to your work. You will

also find that because you are treating yourself with patience, generosity, and respect, you naturally treat others better.

You can become a sacred activist now. You must first actively reveal your intention in awakening the world to oneness. You can do this in many ways, but one way is to go to humanitysteam.com and sign its petition to the United Nations. Next, find opportunities to volunteer using your gifts, your wisdom, or your work toward oneness. Explore and participate in other like-mined organizations and initiatives. Search your heart and ask that these organizations show up in your life. Take simple yet profound action to awaken the world to oneness every day. Send blessings, meditations, and prayers to the media, religious leaders, politicians, corporations, and teachers, and also let them know how you feel about the issues we're facing that divide us and move us away from oneness. Last, get together with other vital, provocative, and creative people and share your thoughts, ideas, and motivations.

People all over the world are rediscovering their ability to shape-shift the world. From the Arab Spring to the cultural creatives, and even to the people of Iceland bravely and smartly saying, "This is not our financial mess and we refuse to pay for it,"—allowing their country to default and causing the government to fail, a situation that seems to be working out quite well for their citizens—people are beginning to wake up to the light. And on the other side, the darkness of the patriarchy fiercely struggles to hold onto what it has claimed over the past five thousand years. As I write this, the Occupy Wall Street movement is gaining strength and spreading all over the United States and into Europe. Is it possible that we've found the hundredth monkey? The battle with the patriarchy, the world elite, is the ultimate battle for the control of this planet. It's time to get down and boogie with the light and the dark that live within each of us that is not us (and is us) and let it move us to do what we can and what needs to be done—and then maybe do a little more.

Chapter 12: Emergence of the Integral Warrior: We Are the Ones We've Been Waiting For

You have been telling the people that this is the Eleventh Hour; now you must go back and tell the people that this is THE HOUR. And there are things to be considered…

Where are you living?
What are you doing?
What are your relationships?
Where is your water?
Are you in right relation? Know your garden.
It is time to speak your Truth.
Create your community.
Be good to each other.
And do not look outside yourself for the leader.
We are the ones we've been waiting for.

Then he clasped his hands together, smiled, and said, "This could be a good time! There is a river flowing now very fast. It is so great and swift that there are those who will be afraid. They will try to hold on to the shore. They will feel they are being torn apart and will suffer greatly. Know the river has its destination. The elders say we must let go of the shore, push off into the middle of the river, keep our eyes open, and our heads above the water. And I say, see who

> *is in there with you and celebrate. At this time in history, we are*
> *to take nothing personally. Least of all, ourselves. For the moment*
> *that we do, our spiritual growth and journey comes to a halt. The*
> *time of the lone wolf is over. Gather yourselves! Banish the word*
> struggle *from your attitude and your vocabulary. All that we do*
> *now must be done in a sacred manner and in celebration.*

> *"We are the ones we've been waiting for."*—Oraibi, Arizona Hopi
> Nation

IN THE CONTEXT OF the Integral Warrior workshop series that I have created and facilitate, all of the processes contained within this book are carefully arranged and covered over multiple two—or four—day weekends. This unfolding is planned and scheduled but can shift according to the needs of the group of men who are involved in the process. Though the path may slightly change from group to group, it is the end destination that is important: that of the freedom contained within surrendering to each and every moment and knowing that we find our self-worth in our sacred purpose, not in external causation.

It doesn't mean that we aren't pleased when our work is acknowledged, validated, and appreciated. It means that we understand that, however big or small our impact is, we know that what we do enters the collective consciousness and that it's all part of our growth, culturally, systematically, physically, and spiritually.

And we must grow in all of these areas or we will leave out essential pieces of our consciousness. We're creating a new way to do "religion," which is inevitable and which Auribindo calls "a spiritual religion of humanity."

A New Integral Spirituality and Integral Religion

An integral religion? Heaven forbid (pun intended)! I can hear all the people wounded by religion in past lives and today saying, "No way," especially many at scientific rational (orange) and pluralistic (green) levels of consciousness.

But religion is not going away, and whatever claims we make around "spiritual, not religious," anyone else looking in is going to consider it religion. So what would the next step in the evolution of religion look like? It certainly won't be the gods of nature or tribalism—not that those still don't exist within the levels of consciousness that created them. Nor will it be the wrathful power god of the Old Testament, the mythic god of an absolutist consciousness, a rejection of anything metaphysical by the rational/scientific level of consciousness, or a sensitive new-age egalitarian deity that says we make everything up as we go, locked in a *pre-trans fallacy*[113] of magic and myth.

A religion that would be considered integral must first set up some parameters of that emerging religion. By definition, integral religion must marry east and west, science and religion, Eros (ascent, many to the one) and Logos (descent, one to the many), and Eros (the masculine) and Agape (the feminine), and much, much more.

Here is a quote from Aurobindo in the *Ideal of Human Unity*:

> A spiritual religion of humanity is the hope of the future ... A religion of humanity means the growing realization that there is a secret Spirit, a divine Reality, in which we are all one, that humanity is its highest present vehicle on earth, that the human race and the human being are the means by which it will progressively reveal itself here. It implies a growing attempt to live out this knowledge and bring about a kingdom of this divine Spirit upon earth. By its growth within us oneness with our fellow-men will become the leading principle of all our life, not merely a principle of cooperation but a deeper brotherhood, a real and an inner sense of unity and equality and a common life.[114]

Whether we ascend to the apex of consciousness, whatever "enlightenment" may be, through meditative practice or through service to Spirit's teleological drive toward emancipation, we are all participants in a single spiritual evolution, and we are all playing a part, even when

---

113   Since both prerational states and transrational states are, in their own ways, nonrational, they appear similar or even identical to the untutored eye and can be mistaken for each other.

114   Twin Lakes, WI: Lotus Light Publications, 1999, p. 307 (July 1918).

we ignore it, refuse to acknowledge it, or think we don't play a part. In integral religion, it is wholeness that we always seek: the integral embrace of immanence with transcendence, of ascent with descent, of humanity with God, and of enlightenment with the divine within all.

My sense is that integral religion isn't something that we can decide to do or not do, validate or invalidate; it's something we *must* do if we are to lay claim to the term *integral*, and it is already emerging. It is time for us to grow up. An integral religion must be grounded in pluralism, and an emerging religion must transcend and include religions of the past, which means that there will be integral Christianity, integral Judaism, integral Buddhism, integral Islam, and on and on, each honoring the other and understanding that each has a piece of the truth and that no religion has all of the truth. All gain from looking at their religion through the broader integral lens.

While fundamentalism militantly expresses it self in various religious forms around the world and here in the United States, others are struggling to reassess their religious traditions—traditions and visions of God that were born of a different time. In other words, many of us are trying to find new ways to be religious.

A verse in the Qur'an says, "Therein God will not change the state of the people unless they change the state of their own selves." An integral spirituality means we participate in divinity and that our own evolution is the evolution of God.

In a conversation I had with Ken Wilber several years ago, he pointed out that the leading edge of progressive consciousness today is turquoise (second tier), a self that goes beyond ego and individuality. Maybe fifty, a hundred, or even a thousand years from now, this "second-tier consciousness" will be the conservative viewpoint, and the leading edge at that time will look back and smile. Hopefully, they will bless us for our efforts as we bless those who came before us, laying the groundwork for this new consciousness as we do the best we can do.

But like today's conservatives, blue and orange (first-tier consciousness that was once the leading edge), we pioneers, stumbling and erring, will have laid down the framework for that new leading edge, perhaps an integral religion.

In the meantime, one of our responsibilities at the current leading edge is to create tension that compels and challenges others to meet us at higher and deeper levels. We can't be wimps about it.

The Four Initiations Revisited

As pointed out in Chapter 9, much of this personal and evolutionary freedom comes from balancing the four primary Jungian archetypes— the King, Warrior, Magician, and Lover. Once we're able to integrate all four into our being, we're able to live and love, ascend and descend, and do and be at will as is called for in each moment, and the initiations of the four archetypes are crucial as the building blocks of the human self.

Robert Moore, coauthor of the *King, Warrior, Magician, Lover* series of books, is credited with decoding the four archetypal foundations of masculinity, and his theory of masculinity has become the most prominent men's theory in international men's work and masculine psychology. Moore says that if we are unaware of the significance of being male and the unique structures of the male psyche that make men so vulnerable to becoming abusers of power, we are very likely to abuse that power and not put it into service to the world. Young men are particularly at risk of abusing masculine power and can be very dangerous if they have not been helped to mature psychologically and spiritually. Uninitiated masculinity is at the heart of most of the planet's problems as a result of uninitiated boys growing up and turning into "monster boys," a parody of what masculinity is supposed to be.

Cultures throughout the ages have known the importance of initiation and ritual in young men's lives, and we've lost our way. The initiation process, or the redemption of masculinity, is a moral imperative critical to all the great hopes we have for justice and peace, that the earth might be fair, and essential for salvaging the great things about masculinity and the importance of being an optimal man in a world that must have awakened men for us to survive as a species.

Each of the four primary archetypes must be initiated. One initiation for all is not enough. This integrated system of care is essential to bring men to optimum male wholeness. These include the capacities of the heart, forceful assertiveness, and becoming a wise man and a generative man worthy of a royal figure. Attention to each of these archetypal systems also requires a fifth element: commitments that transcend the ego, or the transpersonal. The Integral Warrior, and all effective men's work, must steward this process.

Preparing for Emergence

When going through the processes contained within this book, an amazing thing happens. Working with the light and the dark of each of the archetypes reveals to each man his shadow elements and, within those, his sacred work, or *purpose,* is often uncovered. During the last weekend of the Integral Warrior workshops, using all of the awareness they've gained and honed over the months-long process, the men create a sacred ceremony in which they can be witnessed by friends and family who honor them. Each man prepares a vision statement and a mission statement, which include an announcement of their purpose, their gift to the world, is, and how they will bring that gift to their loved ones, their relationships, their work, and the world.

The men are the ones who plan and prepare the emergence ceremony. Using their ability to create sacred space and deciding what they want the ceremony to look like—including an altar, maybe ritual clothing and music—they also prepare their intention statements, which will provide the basis for their self-proclamations as Integral Warriors and Shamanic Priests.

Ideas for creating an initiation intention statement include using or creating a personal mission statement (like those in Stephen Covey's *Seven Habits* books)—for example,

> "I walk the masculine path of Intention, focused on holding space for the Divine Feminine, creating peace and love everywhere I go" (mission statement).

> "As a Shamanic Priest, I am the embodiment of the new

masculine, a wellspring of beauty, love, peace, and purpose as I walk the Path of the Integral Warrior."

This could be a statement complete in and of itself or the beginning of a series of statements covering all of the aspects you intend to expand into. As always, the easiest way to create an intention statement is to keep an open heart and surrender to something larger than your ego. You can do this alone or with a group of similar-hearted men. Some ideas follow:

- Create a ceremony at a special, designated time to be with yourself, your thoughts, and your dreams. Say a prayer, center, and let your heart speak to you.

- Brainstorm to list words that represent what you'd like to create in your life and start there.

- Envision yourself as your highest self and use the qualities that self entails as the foundation of your intention statement.

- Use your favorite embodied man as your guide, or ask your spirit guides, angels, ancestors, or whatever to guide you. Let the words flow from your soul onto the paper.

- Try some free-form writing. Write three pages, without stopping to check your spelling, grammar, or thoughts. You may be surprised at what flows out from you.

- Let this be an organic process. Allow your heart to tell you how to present your new masculine self.

- Let your statement be poetry, not "just" a statement.

- Other questions that may assist you are these:

  - What do you bring into your spiritual life?

  - What aspects of your feminine do you want to include or activate?

  - What places of conflict, discord, or disharmony are

you wanting to bring healing into, both in your life and in your world?

- How do you want to step into your personal spiritual power, and what would you like to manifest with your power?

What would your life look like if there were no barriers to you being your ultimate man, whoever and whatever you wanted to be? How do you want to be physically, spiritually, emotionally, and mentally? Do you know what your life mission is? Why are you here, and what is it that you're supposed to do in the world? What would that look like in your everyday walk in the world?

This first step in preparing for your emergence as the new masculine will take a lot of soul searching, prayer, openness, thought, and time. Take your time. Allow your soul and your spirit into it so that it truly expresses who you are and who you want to be.

Preparing for Your Self-Proclamation Statement

After spending the necessary time and effort to lay the groundwork, it's finally here: the self-proclamation statement in which you claim your highest self and determine how you will bring that highest self to the world.

No one can cause your emergence but you, just as no one can help a caterpillar emerge as a butterfly after going through all the transformative goo. Your statement is a self-proclamation. You, standing in your power, claim the new masculine. No one can do it for you. The container? You created it. The sacred space? You cocreated it with Spirit and your brothers. Your intentions? You manifest them daily by the work you've done to prepare for this moment, this time, this shift, this rebirth.

In shamanic terms, you are consciously dying to the old and being reborn to the new. Sound familiar? It should. It's the basis of all transformational work of all the wisdom traditions and religions that ever existed, whether it's Christian baptism in all its various forms; reincarnation; believing in an afterlife, karma, or past lives; or just a connection to the collective unconscious, and on and on. It also happens to us in our present lives. Unless we get stuck, we are constantly dying to old belief systems and being reborn into new ones. Now we can consciously participate in the death and rebirth process and our own evolution.

Using what you wrote in your intention statement, begin to hone the process using this guide:

Preparing Your Self-Proclamation as an Integral Warrior and a Shamanic Priest

1) Use your Integral Warrior name (chosen when reintegrating the King archetype)

Examples: *I am _____ the shaman of transformation (or Shamanic Priest Charles)*, Laughing White Horse, etc.

2) Choose a primary archetype to align with.

Examples: I *am the shaman of transformation, aligning with the archetype of the magician ...*

3) Highlight descriptive words and phrases from your Integral Warrior notes and journal that really resonate with you and that describe your own unique archetypal nature, your essence, and/or your archetypal self.

Examples: laser-beam focused energy, light-hearted inspiration, man in full, bringer of radical revolutionary life-force energy, cocreator of inspired relationship, holder of space for the Divine Feminine, the new masculine, etc.

4) Possible descriptions (again, open your heart and tune in to whatever wants to come forth)

The new masculine

Laser-beam focused energy

Light-hearted inspiration

Bringer of radical revolutionary life-force energy

Cocreator of inspired relationship

Holder of space for the Divine Feminine

5) Group them together so that you can combine them and condense them into meaningful, articulate, poetic descriptions.

Examples: the new masculine with laser-beam focused energy, holder of space for the Divine Feminine

6) Attach present-tense verbs to the groups, such as the following:

Manifest(ing)

Reveal(ing)

Cocreate(ing)

Embody(ing)

Become(ing)

Cultivate(ing)

Inspire(ing)

Foster(ing)

Synthesize(ing)

Integrate(ing)

Seed(ing)

Harmonize(ing)

7) String together the descriptive phrases and the verbs.

Example: cultivating the new masculine with laser-beam focused energy, holder of space for the Divine Feminine

8) State clearly your newfound or reinforced purpose, what your gift is

to the world, and how the process has changed you or enabled you to move to a new stage in your life.

9) Find one or more concluding purposes.

> Example: Integrating the four archetypes, inspiring and modeling the new masculine with my presence, my gifts to the world, to serve my loved ones, humankind and the planet

10) I am Shamanic Priest Gary Laughing White Horse, aligned with the archetype of the Magician, driven by the Warrior, tempered by the Lover, cultivating the King's big-picture awareness of the new masculine with laser-beam focused energy, holder of space for the Divine Feminine, integrating the four archetypes, inspiring and modeling the new masculine with my presence, my gifts to the world, and my sacred activism, to serve my loved ones, humankind and the planet and the evolution of consciousness ...

Fried by the Feminine

A little over a year ago, the most amazing woman I'd ever met came into my life. I'd always liked strong women, but she was clearly the strongest woman I'd ever seen: powerful, capable, courageous, loving, and with fully embodied feminine and masculine aspects. Today she is my beloved, and we're on the way to building our life and future together.

I believe that the reason this woman came into my life and that I was able to step up to her and her power is because, a few years ago, I decided I had to be the kind of man that a woman like this would be attracted to. I had to fully step into my own power, and that meant doing my own work, not just sitting by and letting life take me, but by me taking charge of my life and my own embodied masculine. When both of us do our own work, it helps us support each other in the directions that most serve our growth in love, relationship, manifestation, and happiness.

Your woman is going through some inevitable changes in her life. She chose you, she wants you to join her in this growth, and she

> *wants your support and your strength. It's the greatest gift you can give her.*

I wrote this a few years ago at Anyaa's request. She was writing an article on how the masculine can support their feminine partners as they go through the Shamanic Priestess process she facilitates for women all over the world. She had asked men who have successfully supported their women through this transformative process to support other men who are now going through what they went through with a couple of written paragraphs she could share.

A T-shirt that I created and sell on one of my websites[115] says, "Enlightenment ain't cheap." It's a dual meaning: yes, we pay a lot of money to attend workshops and so forth, but we sometimes also pay for our transformation with our relationships; our jobs; and our blood, sweat, and tears. Many men are frightened that their relationships with their women are going to change as a result of this process, and they will change. But I refer you back to my quote above and challenge you to give her that gift.

One of the responses she got was from a man who objected to the duality of masculine and feminine approaches to conscious evolution, and I understand that once one has attained the ability to rest in the nondual, the masculine and feminine dissolve into "the One." People can even attain the nondual in altered states—those temporary states we talked about earlier in the book—before they reach that rare stage consciousness in which nonduality can be embodied.

But until we get past the state experiences and into later stage structures, there is a natural hierarchy that must be obeyed—we have to be careful not to confuse natural hierarchies with dominator hierarchies. One of the steps in this hierarchy is going through and healing our masculine and feminine selves. Women have thousands of years of domination by the masculine that they generally have to work through before they're able to begin to step into their true power, and this work, at this level, cannot be taught by men any more than the same work for men can be fully led by a woman. Once we've done this work of healing our core

---

115   The iBoutique, https://www.cafepress.com/iboutique

childhood wounds around the masculine and feminine, then either men or women can take over from there, but not until the healing has been faced, met, and completed.

So to get to the later state-stage structures, especially the nondual, it's critical that the masculine and feminine work be completed because if it's not, we bring the ego and shadow aspects of those qualities with us to trick us, harass us, and fool us into thinking we've made it when we really haven't.

So for the men who fear the work that their women are doing, do your own work and step up to who she's becoming, or at least support her because she's becoming with or without you. Here's what one woman said after her husband returned from the introductory weekend of the Integral Warrior workshop:

> *"The synchronicities of this past weekend were just profound. First of all, he LOVED Gary's workshop. I noticed a change in his demeanor and energy just from the first weekend. And connecting with the men and himself in that way is what he has been really desiring and missing in his life. It took all my strength NOT to jump up and down and squeal when he told me all about it, and about how he identified with the "King"… continuing to talk about how much he saw pieces of himself in a way that he could actually understand. My heart just fluttered as it felt so incredibly good to have this opportunity to hear him speak from his heart … and witness the changes!! Gary really set an example for him. He also found the Shadow work to be very revealing to him … He said he could see much of the shadow of the 'King' to be much of what he experienced of his own father … To be able to communicate in this way with him has been more than a miracle."*

One of the pivotal moments in my relationship life, as I was searching for conscious partnership, was the realization that, in order to attract the kind of partner I wanted in my life, I had to be the kind of partner such a person would be attracted to.

And for those who think we can get to enlightenment in a single, sudden gift of a leap in consciousness or realization without doing the work—and it apparently does happen, but rarely—for most of us, there are many, many paths to the nondual, or what is called "enlightenment," and most of them require that we step into the fires of transformation and let them burn away what's holding us back. Denial of those different paths and the serious and necessary work that needs to be done is "spiritual bypassing," or worse, enlightened fundamentalism.

Summary

As long as human beings have walked on this earth, we have been trying to put things together, to figure out how everything works. We've pretty much done the best we could given our stages of development, our physical world, our cultures, and the structures that supported them. Now it's time for us to do better.

As I stated earlier—for the first time in our history, we now have access to all of the combined wisdom traditions, philosophies, religions, and ideas that came before us. The synthesis of all of these spiritual, philosophical, and wisdom traditions and knowledge is allowing us to create new paradigms of thought, understanding, and spirituality.

As we move away from fundamentalist thinking and intellectual totalitarianism, we invite in and open up whole new ways of thinking and being. Beyond moving men from old stages to new stages, *Integral Shamanism, Awakening the New Masculine,* and the Integral Warrior encourage, teach, and demand that men strive for intellectual and spiritual honesty—claiming the two-million-year-old intellectual mind that is their birthright—and dig deep into their hearts and minds for both the cognitive and experiential wisdom that has the potential to create a new worldview—an integral worldview—starting from existing worldviews, morphing and shape-shifting into something different.

It is one of the oldest songs on the planet and, indeed, in the universe: evolution in all its forms. From the splitting of cells, to individuals, to relationships, to social systems, to civilizations, to the cosmos, each evolutionary movement is preceded by differentiation and reunification and results in increasing complexities. You are part of the tipping point that moves us into this new way of being as the old ways fall away, and it doesn't matter what you call it or if you ascribe to it—the great shift, the turning of the ages, the collapse, the planetary dark night of the soul, the end of patriarchy. There is an ascension process taking place on the planet, a move toward unity consciousness, and it is birthing a new earth. Today, as all of the old systems collapse under the weight of the dying paradigm of infinite growth and the capitalism that came with it, we stand on the precipice of a new beginning, new systems, and a new human, and like the old scribes just before the invention of the printing press, we have no idea what that will all look like. We do know, one way or another, that everything is about to change.

That's a lot to hold, but that's exactly what is being asked of us—to hold this "vast terrain of consciousness within our own consciousness, to hold tension of the opposites, so that we can come all the way through these times to a new world on the other side. The more beings that have eyes to see, and ears to hear what is happening, the closer we get to the Tipping Point that gives us the momentum we need for the ride through to the other side. And what a ride it is!" [116]

The time is now. Don't be afraid to step into the power you feel within you. It is part of your sacred work to serve in these times. You chose to be here at this time. You are in good company with all of the others who are waking up to their expanding capacities. We have hit the boundaries of population and resources but not of possibilities. The Integral Warrior—and what it represents for men who are waking up—is part of a larger grand synthesis taking place all over the planet. There's nowhere to go but forward in a never-ending evolution of consciousness.

---

116   Anyaa McAndrew, "Goddess on the Loose" blog, August 2011.

Certainty

*Certainty undermines one's power, and turns happiness
into a long shot. Certainty confines.*

*Dears, there is nothing in your life that will
not change—especially your ideas of God.*

*Look what the insanity of righteous knowledge can do:
crusade and maim thousands
in wanting to convert that which
is already gold
into gold.*

*Certainty can become an illness
that creates hate and
greed.*

God once said to Tuka,

*"Even I am ever changing—
I am ever beyond
Myself,*

*what I may have once put my seal upon,
may no longer be
the greatest
Truth."*

—Tukaram [117]

---

117   http://www.panhala.net/Archive/Certainty.html

RECOMMENDED READING

(IN ALPHABETICAL ORDER)

Carolyn Baker, *Sacred Demise: Walking the Spiritual Path of Industrial Civilization's Collapse* (Bloomington, IN: iUniverse, 2009).

Don Edward Beck and Christopher Crown, *Spiral Dynamics: Mastering Values, Leadership, and Change* (Oxford, UK: Blackwell Publishing, 1996).

Pema Chodren, *Start Where You Are: A Guide to Compassionate Living* (Boston: Shambhala Classics, 2001).

Allan Combs, *The Radiance of Being: Understanding the Grand Integral Vision; Living the Integral Life,* Second Edition (St. Paul, MN: Paragon House, 2002).

David Deida, *The Way of the Superior Man: A Spiritual Guide to Mastering the Challenges of Women, Work, and Sexual Desire* (Boulder, CO: Sounds True, Inc. 2004).

Jared Diamond, *Collapse: How Societies Choose to Fail or Succeed* (The Penguin Group, 2005).

Matthew Fox, *The Hidden Spirituality of Men: Ten Metaphors to Awaken the Sacred Masculine* (Novato, CA: New World Library, 2007).

Joseph Gelfer, *Numen, Old Men: Contemporary Masculine Spiritualities and the Problem of Patriarchy* (Sheffield, UK: Equinox Publishers, 2009).

Andrew Harvey, *The Hope: A Guide to Sacred Activism* (Hay House, 2009)

David R. Hawkins, MD, PhD, *Power vs. Force: The Hidden Determinants of Human Behavior* (Carlsbad, CA: Hay House, 2002).

Richard Heinberg, *The End of Growth: Adapting to Our New Economic Reality* (Gabriola Island, BC, Canada: New Society Publishers, 2011).

His Holiness the Dalai Lama and Howard C. Cutler, M.SD., *The Art of Happiness: A Handbook for Living* (New York: Riverhead Books, 1998).

David Korten, *The Great Turning: From Empire to Earth Community* (Bloomfield, CT: Kumarian Press, Inc.; San Francisco: Berret-Koehler Publishers, Inc., 2006).

George Leonard and Michael Murphy, *The Life We Are Given* (New York: G.P. Putnam's Sons, 1995).

Robert Augustus Masters, *Spiritual Bypassing: When Spirituality Disconnects from What Really Matters* (North Atlantic Books: Berkely, CA, 2010).

Dennis Genpo Merzel, *Big Mind, Big Heart: Finding Your Way* (Maclean, VA: Big Mind Publishing, 2007).

Dan Millman, *Way of the Peaceful Warrior: A Book That Changes Lives* (Tiburon, CA: H.J. Kramer, Inc., 1980).

Robert Moore and Douglas Gillette, *King, Warrior, Magician, Lover: Rediscovering the Archetypes of the Mature Masculine* (San Francisco: HarperCollins, 1991). (Also, for a deeper look at each the archetypes, see the complete series of four books, one on each archetype.)

John Perkins, *Shape Shifting: Techniques for Global and Personal Transformation* (Rochester, VT: Destiny Books, 1997).

Richard Rohr, *Adam's Return: The Five Promises of Male Initiation* (New York: Crossroad Publishing Company, 2004).

Peter Senge, C. Otto Scharmer, Joseph Jaworski, and Betty Sue Flowers, *Presence: Human Purpose and the Field of the Future* (Cambridge, MA: Society for Organizational Living, 2004).

Tony Schwartz, *What Really Matters: Searching for Wisdom in America* (New York: Bantam Books, 1995).

Linda Star Wolf, *Shamanic Breathwork: Journeying Beyond the Limits of the Self* (Rochester, VT: Bear & Co., 2009).

Roger Walsh, MD, PhD, *The World of Shamanism: New Views of an Ancient Tradition* (Woodsbury, MN: Llewellyn Publications, 2010).

John Welwood, *Journey From the Heart: The Path of Conscious Love* (HarperCollins, 1990).

Ken Wilber, *A Brief History of Everything* (Boston: Shambhala Publications, 2007).

Also recommended is anything and everything by Ken Wilber, but especially the following, and all can be found on Amazon.com:

> *Grace and Grit*
> *A Theory of Everything*
> *One Taste*
> *Integral Spirituality*
> *The Essential Ken Wilber*
> *The Integral Vision*

Ken Wilber, Terry Patten, Adam Leonard, and Marco Morelli, *Integral Life Practice* (Boston & London: Integral Books, 2008).

INDEX

Loevinger, Jane, 41
Lover, 107–110, 119
    accessing, 108–109
    integrated initiation, 109
    oath as an integrated, 109–110
Luminous energy, 68–70

M

Magician, 110–112, 119
    integrated, 112–113
    oaths and affirmations, 112–113
Mandela, Nelson, 138
Man Enough: Fathers, Sons, and the Search for Masculinity (Pittman), 2
MAN for the ERA. *See* Men Allied Nationally for the Equal Rights Amendment
Mankind Project (MKP), 3, 54, 134
Masculinity. *See also* Integral warrior
    archetypes, 99–120
    behavior and, 18
    colors and, 45–46, 47
    denial of, xxi
    divine, 12
    egotism and, 7–8
    evolution of, 22
    Genesis myth of man, 120
    growth of, 16–25
    men's movement, 6
    mythopoetic men's movement, 2–5
    new masculine, 11–15
    pathways to healing, 1–17
    self-proclamation statement, 152–155
    three stages of, 24–25
    women integrating, 14
Maslow, Abraham, 41
McAndrew, Anyaa, xvii, 1, 84

McCarroll, Robert James, Sr., 110, 117
Meade, Michael J., 2
Meditation, 74, 126–127. *See also* Insight Dialogue
    Buddhist, 74
    inner shaman, 91–93
    Tonglen, 34, 74
Men
    gay spirituality, 6
    liberation, 6
    lifespan, xviii–xix
    men's/father's rights, 6
    traditional male, xx
Men Allied Nationally for the Equal Rights Amendment (MAN for the ERA), 6
Men Overcoming Violence (MOVE), 6
Meta-Shamanism, 80–82
Minnesota Men's Conference, 3
MKP. *See* Mankind Project
Models
    AQAL, 29–33, 44, 95
    developmental, 26–37, 40–46, 42
    five aspects of, 34–37
    new masculine, 21–23
    three-stage, 7–8
Montaigne, 76
Moore, Robert, xxi, 100, 135, 149
Moore, Thomas, xvii
Morality, 122
Mother Earth, 67–68
MOVE. *See* Men Overcoming Violence
Movies, 2
Muscular Christianity, 5
Music, 65
Mythopoetic men's movement, 2–5
    description of, 3

Violence, xviii

Open Book Editions
A Berrett-Koehler Partner

Open Book Editions is a joint venture between Berrett-Koehler Publishers and Author Solutions, the market leader in self-publishing. There are many more aspiring authors who share Berrett-Koehler's mission than we can sustainably publish. To serve these authors, Open Book Editions offers a comprehensive self-publishing opportunity.

A Shared Mission

Open Book Editions welcomes authors who share the Berrett-Koehler mission—Creating a World That Works for All. We believe that to truly create a better world, action is needed at all levels—individual, organizational, and societal. At the individual level, our publications help people align their lives with their values and with their aspirations for a better world. At the organizational level, we promote progressive leadership and management practices, socially responsible approaches to business, and humane and effective organizations. At the societal level, we publish content that advances social and economic justice, shared prosperity, sustainability, and new solutions to national and global issues.

Open Book Editions represents a new way to further the BK mission and expand our community. . We look forward to helping more authors challenge conventional thinking, introduce new ideas, and foster positive change.

For more information, see the Open Book Editions website:
http://www.iuniverse.com/Packages/OpenBookEditions.aspx

Join the BK Community! See exclusive author videos, join discussion groups, find out about upcoming events, read author blogs, and much more! http://bkcommunity.com/